H·E·R·B·S
for Weddings &
Other Celebrations

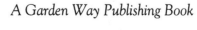

A Treasury of Recipes, Gifts & Decorations

BERTHA REPPERT

A Garden Way Publishing Book

STOREY

Storey Communications, Inc.
Schoolhouse Road
Pownal, Vermont 05261

Edited by Gwen W. Steege

Cover and text design by Cindy McFarland

Cover photographs by Nicholas Whitman

Text photographs by Cindy McFarland, except where indicated

Text production by Michelle Arabia

Line drawings by Brigita Fuhrmann, except pages 5, 11, 81 (bottom), 95, 120, 137, 139, 140, 145, 149, 152, 157, 160 by Charles H. Joslin; pages 23, 48, 55 (top), 68, 73, 74, 75, 83, 84, 86, 90, 108, 124, 125, 179 by Marjorie Reppert; page 50 by Alison Kolesar; and page 51 by Paula Winchester

Lyrics from "Sunrise, Sunset" from Fiddler on the Roof, page 10 used with permission: Copyright Renewed 1993 Mayerling Productions Ltd. and Jerry Bock

Indexed by Northwind Editorial Services

Copyright © 1993 by Bertha Reppert

Garden Way Publishing was founded in 1973 as part of the Garden Way Incorporated Group of Companies, dedicated to bringing gardening information and equipment to as many people as possible. Today the name "Garden Way Publishing" is licensed to Storey Communications, Inc., in Pownal, Vermont. For a complete list of Garden Way Publishing titles, call 1-800-827-8673. Garden Way Incorporated manufactures products in Troy, New York, under the Troy-Bilt® brand including garden tillers, chipper/shredders, mulching mowers, sicklebar mowers, and tractors. For information on any Garden Way Incorporated product, please call 1-800-345-4454.

Printed in the United States by Courier
Text color printing by Excelsior Printing Company
First printing, November 1993

Library of Congress Cataloging-in-Publication Data

Reppert, Bertha P., 1919–
   Herbs for weddings and other celebrations : a treasury of recipes, gifts, and decorations / Bertha Reppert.
        p.   cm.
     "A Garden Way Publishing book."
     Includes bibliographical references (p.   ) and index.
     ISBN 0-88266-866-8 (hc) — ISBN 0-88266-864-1 (pb)
     1. Cookery (Herbs)   2. Herbs—Utilization.   3. Wedding decora-
tions.   4. Flower arrangement. I. Title.
  TX819.H4R52   1993
  745.594'1—dc20   92-56147
                                             CIP

Dedicated to
all brides,
everywhere —yesterday's, today's, tomorrow's
(two million a year!)
and to
all brides
who know that in matters of the **Heart** *and the* **Hearth**
"Herbs Make the Difference"

Table of Contents

Thank-You Note

I seem always beholden to good friends and loving family who pitch in to help on my many projects. This book is no exception. Besides hugs and kisses to Byron, my patient helpmate of four decades plus, I am so very grateful to Rosina, Frances, several Helens, Vicki, Gary, Colleen, Susanna, Katy, Sharon, Holly, Nancy, Minga, Theresa, Marjorie, Carol, Carolynn, Scott, Hildegard, Emily, and a host of others who shall be nameless, even to me. Who knows the origin of a great idea or recipe? This little herbal handbook for brides is built on a pyramid of such inspiration as well as the bounty from my herb garden.

And a special thanks to all the brides who allowed me to be a part of their weddings.
To the best of my knowledge all the knots are still tied and herbs deserve a lot of the credit.

XXOO
Bertha

PART I

Herbs
Make the Difference

Every part of the happy preparations for a wedding
can — indeed should — include herbs. Be it a simple ceremony before the fireplace at home or an elaborate processional in a lofty cathedral, the scent and beauty and symbolism
of herbs make them eminently suitable. This book is filled with
suggestions for creative ways for you to share your rightful place
in the spotlight with herbs. Indeed, there are enough ideas here
for several prospective new households! Pick and choose
the ones that suit your lifestyle best, and build upon
the suggestions with your own improvisations.

Planning a Herbal Wedding

F OR A TRULY MEMORABLE WEDDING, let herbs do the work for you, help you lay your plans, and pleasantly see them through to a most satisfactory conclusion. Your wedding will linger in everyone's memory for years — unto the next generation. Believe me!

Whether for food or decoration, you can use fresh, dried, or pressed herbs in any quantity available to you. If you have a herb garden, that's splendid; but if not, don't let that stop you from planning a herbal wedding. Herbs can be purchased at farmers' markets (ask for bunches of sage, mint, and other common herbs, then place an order), or from local gardeners, members of garden clubs, and herb or health food shops. Even supermarkets now carry many fresh herbs, or you can use dried herbs and spices sold in bottles and tins for seasoning. Sometimes cooperative florists can get the herbs you are seeking, especially fresh bay, rosemary, or myrtle, which may have to be flown in from warmer climates.

Speaking of the powers of rosemary . . . it overtoppeth all the flowers in the garden.

— Robert Hackett, 1607

Mail-order sources of fresh herbs are listed on pages 181-182. These are reputable herb growers who know how to condition and pack fresh herbs for shipping. Write to request prices. Rest assured that for this once-in-a-lifetime event that will be the "talk of the town" fresh herbs flown in are well worth their price.

How to Begin: Planning a Theme and Colors

Whether you are putting together a new outfit to wear, redecorating a room, planning your holiday season decorations, or setting up a year's program for a successful club, a specific theme helps you accomplish your project more easily and more effectively. In orchestrating your wedding — from announcements to thank-you notes — a theme is your salvation. Let herbs be your special thread, woven through all the festivities and formalities, tying everything together.

Begin your plans by choosing a color harmony. This could be your favorite colors (blue, pink, or purple) or those dictated by the season (russet or gold in fall, garnet and off-white at Christmas), or (something terribly old and now considered smartly modern) an "all-white" wedding. Make your choice and then stick to it by coordinating all your plans around these colors. Once the decision is made, many tasks are easier, and the total impact will be smashing.

Next, decide what your theme will be besides herbs. For instance, if you collect stuffed teddy bears or adore roses, have shelves of English cottages, think butterflies are the loveliest of God's creations, can't resist antique baskets, have a collection of dolls from around the world, or enjoy seashells, incorporate these objects into your plans. "Favorite things" make a most charming theme — especially when combined with herbs. (See color photo, page 91)

Once you have chosen a color and a theme, you may decide to limit your choice of herbs to just one, such as rosemary, "for remembrance." Let's take an example and think of parsley as an herbal theme. You will be amazed at the many ways it can be incorporated into your festivities. Have you ever looked closely at a bunch of parsley? It is a bouquet all by itself. A brilliant dark green leaf curled into ruffled convolutions, glowing with health, it symbolizes "victory," "festivity," and "joy." Parsley mixes beautifully with wedding flowers and thus can be used in centerpieces as well as for a lavish garnish. Press and tuck it into invitations, announcements, and thank-you notes. It might be a good idea to write up parsley in the wedding program. Or you may choose to use a trio of herbs — parsley, sage, and angelica, for example. My preference, however, is to use an assortment of herbs.

Wedding Themes

To inspire your thinking about a theme that might have special meaning for you, here are some herbal and other themes that others have used and enjoyed.

A Rosemary Wedding — "That's for Remembrance"

I'm sure the very first wedding bouquets, centuries ago, included rosemary. An ancient symbol of remembrance, rosemary also signifies devotion and loyalty. Its fragrance and association with matters of the head and heart make rosemary ideally suited to weddings. Indeed, it is *the* herb of weddings.

In Yugoslavia, rosemary is pinned on the lapel of all the wedding guests as they enter the house of worship and worn throughout the festivities. In merry old England, the sprigs of rosemary were gilded and then distributed to the guests.

Because rosemary is symbolic of love and loyalty, English bridesmaids of years gone by presented the bridegroom with a bunch of it on his wedding morning. Wouldn't today's groom be astounded by such a ceremony? A sprig of rosemary was always included in bridal bouquets, to ensure happiness and good luck. Branches of rosemary also were used to decorate

Rosemary

the halls and churches during the wedding and burned as incense during the religious service.

In Mexico, rosemary is grown as a good-luck charm. Referred to as "she," the plant is tended as protection against witches and their deviltry. Recently, an exchange student from Mexico told of being given pieces from the sacred rosemary plant to pack in her luggage for a safe return journey home by train. A companion didn't get any for her trip home, however, because she was flying; since witches don't travel on planes, the family considered it unnecessary! Be sure to pack rosemary in your going-away suitcase.

Rosemary's Wedding

When a girl named Rosemary, whose initials happened to be R.U.E., got married, guess her herbal theme! Right. Lots of rosemary for remembrance, and rue, Shakespeare's herb of grace. Because the wedding was in the dead of winter, we elected to dry a great deal of rosemary, rue ('Blue Beauty'), and lavender (for luck), as well as many other herbs and a host of little 'Fairy' roses to create a nosegay bouquet and halo for the bride and bridesmaids — bouquets from the summer harvest. (For instructions on how to create a bride's halo, see pages 49-50.) Using moss-covered floral foam and lace doilies, the fragile herbs and flowers along with a cloud of fresh baby's-breath and a host of ribbons were easily transformed into many wedding arrangements. After the ceremony, they were enjoyed as dried decorations for many years, treasured keepsakes still speaking their herbal messages eloquently, "to have and to hold" forever.

Lots o' Lace Wedding

Nostalgia, sentiment, old-fashioned traditions — if this is your dream of a wedding, do it with lace. Buy yards and yards of lacy-look material and a bolt of 3-inch lace to use on everything. Seek out lacelike paper napkins, lacy invitations, paper doilies. Grandmother's old-fashioned laces are treasures you may be able to use. Here are a few more ideas:

Use pots of rosemary to glorify your wedding. Line the steps of the church or synagogue, edge the aisle, ornament the chancel, decorate the reception hall, and use them as favors. Such a wedding reaps special blessings.

Rosemary is for remembrance
Between us day and night.
Wishing that I might always have
You present in my sight.

—Thomas Robinson, A Nosegay for Lovers, 1584

- Make simple squares of lace to cover tops of tables.

- For favors, stitch up small lace pouches to fill with potpourri.

- For even simpler sachets, use narrow satin ribbon to tie up 6-inch squares of lace.

- Carry a lace-bedecked nosegay — perhaps tied to a lacy parasol.

- Glue a bit of lace on one side of the invitation.

- Wrap the bridesmaids' gifts in lacy-look paper.

- Use paper doilies under everything, including the candles and centerpieces.

- Tuck lace into the bouquets and the wreaths on the door.

- Make a lavishly lacy ring pillow.

- Wear lace, of course!

Your wedding will be very special and beautiful beyond words, from the announcements to the thank-you notes, if you lace it lavishly.

Lacy thank-you notes. Buy plain notepapers and matching envelopes. Cut a lace heart out of paper or cloth. Using white glue thinned with an equal amount of water, glue the heart on the front of the notepaper. When the glue is dry, press your notepapers flat with a warm iron — don't lay them on top of each other until dry!

Lacy nosegays. This is an easy, sit-down, summer-fall project, best accomplished while fresh herbs and dried flowers are available in abundance. Easiest to work with while fresh, the herbs will dry in place, creating a fragrant nosegay.

Cut 18-inch pieces of 2- or 3-inch-wide lace. Using easy running stitches, gather one side and pull into a circle with a small center opening. Where the ends meet, overcast the seam.

Using the sources listed in the back of this book, winter brides in cold climates can order all the fresh herbs they want from growers equipped to cut, condition, and ship fresh herbs, second-day air, twelve months of the year.

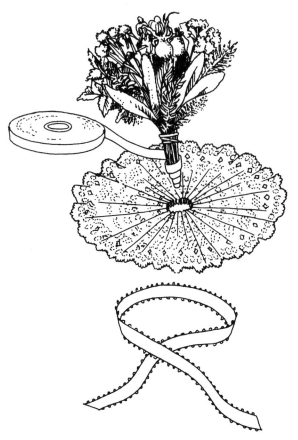

To make a nosegay, gather an 18-inch piece of lace, tape together a bundle of herbs and flowers, insert the stems through the circle of lace, and garnish with a bow.

This takes a few minutes for each nosegay. Put together little bunches of herbs, seed pods, colorful dried flowers, and baby's-breath. Secure the small bunch with a rubber band, and poke it through the center of the lacy circle. Add ribbons if you wish. Wrap the stems with white florist's tape.

Pile the nosegays on a pedestal cake plate — or tiered cake plates — for centerpieces that are also favors. Also, these little nosegays are truly a "thing of beauty" laid on the branches of a Christmas tree; add small gold balls.

Paper lace for nosegays. Buy 8- or 10-inch lace paper doilies. Make small bunches of fresh-from-the-herb-garden fragrant foliage and flowers. Tie about a dozen stems together and insert them through a slit in the center of the paper doily. Use florist's tape to secure herbs and paper. Tape the stems and attach a bow. Keep refrigerated until needed.

Nature's lace. In summer, gather all the snowy Queen-Anne's-lace you can find. Reduce the stems to 2 inches or so. Promptly place flowers in a shoe box with a 1-inch layer of sterilized playbox sand in the bottom. (Sand is available at any hardware store or building supplier. Do not use builder's sand.) Lay the Queen-Anne's-lace blossoms head down, stem up. Cover completely with more sand. In about a week, your beautiful lacy blossoms will be permanently dried, to use as decorations or to be glued on invitations. Spray them with hair spray (add a touch of glitter for a holiday mood, if you wish), and pack them away in plastic-covered boxes, safe from summer's humidity, until needed. They have a fairyland quality when used in bridal bouquets, glued onto garlands, or added to wreaths or Christmas trees.

Do You Know a Field of Daisies?

Daisies — "day's eyes" or the "eye of the day" — are perfect for weddings. If your wedding is in May or June, you may be able to find a meadow filled with daisies that you can use for your wedding. Daisy mums and silk flower daisies are also available all year from the florist. Symbol of innocence, Wordsworth's "bright flowers" are lovely for a wedding and all the prenuptial parties.

Use them lavishly, in every way imaginable — by the basketful — as altar flowers, mother's corsages, on your thank-you notes. Be sure to press some to frame with your invitation, for they express "loyal love." Don't overlook traditional daisy chains, garlands of long-stemmed daisies tied together in a thick

He loves me,
he loves me not,
he loves me,
he loves me not,
he loves me . . . .

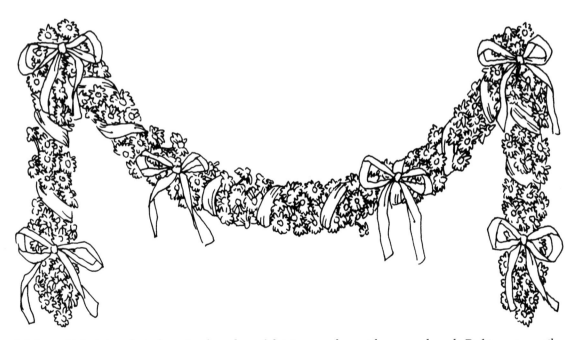

Make a thick daisy chain by tying bunches of daisies together with strong thread. Refrigerate until needed and then decorate with ribbon.

This popular song is now often used as a processional at Jewish weddings, as the bride is escorted down the aisle by her parents and the groom by his parents.

rope. Secure them with stout carpet thread or crochet cotton, and keep them in plastic bags under refrigeration until needed. Then, wrap them artistically with narrow satin ribbon. Use extra ribbon for bows along the chain.

Make your daisy chains in several continuous lengths to crown the bride, to mark pews or aisle seats, to lay along the edge of the head table at the reception, and to wreathe the punch bowl and the wedding cake. The flower girl can start the proceedings by strewing a few daisy flowers in the bride's path, and the bridesmaids, as in a Kate Greenaway print, can carry daisy chains instead of bouquets.

For a unique moment in the ceremony, present each guest with a long-stemmed field daisy, and include a symbolic "tying of the knot." At a given point, each guest will be instructed to tie his or her daisy to those of the neighbors on either side, making one long chain around the room. (Florist flowers have stiff stems, but wildflowers have supple stems, making them a better choice.) The ushers (who, of course, wear daisy boutonnieres) can collect the daisy chain to decorate the reception hall.

Melissa's Wedding

Every woman named Melissa has her very own herb for a built-in theme — lemon balm or *Melissa officinalis*. Its chartreuse foliage in baskets combines richly with field daisies in spring, gold roses in summer, or mums at any time of year. Melissas therefore can use yellow and white as their color theme, baskets as their "favorite things" theme, and lemon balm as their herb theme. How fortunate to be named for a herb!

Melissa can press the leaves to use on her notes; make a tea with the herb; serve it with ginger ale for a party punch with lemon sherbet to make it more festive or with champagne or sherry for the wedding punch — a true Melissa gala (see *Melissa's Punch*).

Melissa is a prolific herb. A few plants of it will dress tables and provide decorations for around the cake (especially *Hawaiian Wedding Cake*) and huge bouquets for the entire wedding party. *Lemon Balm Jelly* makes a delightful favor for a prewedding party (recipes in part II).

Gifts from the Sea

Your favorite old collection of seashells can complement herbs nicely. Pile them down the center of tables, with herbs and flowers here and there, and sand surrounding all. Add vigil lights or candles, too. Pile seashells high with potpourri

Lemon balm

Balm was the main ingredient of the celebrated Carmelite Water, made by the nuns at the abbey of St. Juste six hundred years ago. This became an important addition to the toilet preparations of cultured men and women in Medieval Europe. It is made from 2 pounds of fresh balm leaves;   pound of lemon peel; 2 ounces each of nutmeg, cloves, and coriander, a little cinnamon, and some angelica root. These are placed in a still together with   gallon of orange-flower water and 1 gallon of alcohol, and slowly distilled. The "London Dispensatory" of 1696 said that it would "renew youth," and it was also taken as a restorative cordial.

Pliny and, later, Gerard, recommended rubbing balm leaves on a new hive to make the bees stay, and balm tea was taken by countrymen as a tonic. Culpeper said "it causes the mind and the heart to become merrie." Due to the presence of potassium salts, it is a valuable restorative and gives one a sense of well being.

The chopped leaves make a pleasing addition to a cream cheese sandwich or, used sparingly, to a salad; they add lemon flavor to summer drinks just as borage adds a cucumber flavor to beverages.

— From *Flowers and Herbs of Love* by Roy Genders

or use them as serving dishes for butter pats, individual dips, and sauces; as tea bag holders; or, if you have larger ones, as salad plates, especially for seafood. Stuffed with sprigs of herbs, they become both centerpieces and favors.

With This Ring I Thee Wed

Symbols of eternal and everlasting love, rings — engagement and wedding — dominate the celebration from the moment the couple says "Yes" until they say "I do" — and for all the years of marriage. The symbolism of rings goes back to ancient Egypt, where the circle was the hieroglyph that indicated endless eternity. Rings were a symbol of the ideal marriage, carrying love beyond life. The symbolism of the ring permeates wedding celebrations today, as well.

♥ Fill ring pillows with fragrant dried herbs or potpourri. (See pages 85–86.)

♥ Set the scene with herbal wreaths on the doors of the house of worship or your home. (See pages 69–72.)

♥ Create candle rings for the chancel or for centerpieces

at the reception. Use fresh herbs or dried colorful flowers. (See page 64.)

♥ Tiny honeysuckle rings make ideal napkin rings.

♥ A rosemary halo for the bride's hair is a truly crowning glory. (See pages 49–50.)

Other Ways to Use Herbs

With your themes in mind, you will soon find dozens of ways to include herbs in all parts of your wedding preparations and the big day itself. Let the ideas that follow be a starting point.

Bridal Showers

Shower bouquet. Have handy several yards of narrow white ribbon, a large flat wicker mat, and a bowl of freshly picked mint or other assorted herbs. As the packages are unwrapped, affix all the bows to the wicker mat with the white ribbon. Tuck a little bunch of herbs (4 to 6 sprigs) into the center of each bow and tie securely. After the party, the guests of honor will have a colorful and fragrant door decoration for their new home. The herbs will dry in place and the decoration can be treasured always. It could even be packed away carefully for the tenth anniversary party.

Raise the roof! Build a miniature house of heavy cardboard (a large box will work). Construct it so that the peaked roof lifts off. Paint it white and paste on windows of colored paper. On the side, print the honored couple's names and the wedding date in large letters. Surround the house with bunches of fragrant herbs, such as

As a focal point for the bridal shower gifts, create a miniature cardboard house and surround it with herbs.

There's rosemary, that's for remembrance;
— there's rue for you; and here's some for me;
we may call it, herb o' grace o' Sundays —

— William Shakespeare,
Hamlet

mint, lemon balm, artemisias, costmary, angelica, and so forth. Fill the little house with wrapped gifts for the home.

Personalized tablecloth. Hand-painting fabrics has become a popular, easy, and a fun hobby. To create a personalized tablecloth that will be a treasured keepsake, take a cloth with a white background, purchased or stitched to fit the tables, and use fabric pens to draw the "favorite things" of your wedding theme. You'll find hot pinks, reds, soft greens and lavenders, yellows, oranges, and heavenly blues, so you can be as colorful as you wish or stick to your wedding color scheme. Be sure to "embroider" with your pen all the herbs your party will include, and write out their symbolism. Simple squares are easiest to do. Use table skirts with napkins to match. Perhaps your guests would like to sign their names. (Dover Books has a *Herb Coloring Book* with simple drawings of many herbs; see Mail-Order Sources on pages 181–182.)

Love bath balls. These are fun, perfect Valentine or bridal tokens — both fragrant and "scentimental." They can be tucked into ivy nosegays for color and aroma or just as easily mailed out as invitations along with your message of love. The ingredients are readily available either from your garden, from your pantry shelves, or from your nearest herb shop. See my recipe *Herbs for the Bath* (page 19), which will make a dozen or more darling little bath balls. Don't mislay anything this versatile! In fact, this recipe can double as a Valentine tea or as a filler for sachets. (If you use the mixture for tea, omit the comfrey.)

Decorations, Food, and Gifts

Labelling your herbs. Herbs assume their proper role when people know what they are and why you chose to use them. Let them express the traditional bridal wishes for health, love, and prosperity. If you don't have the most decorative handwriting, perhaps a friend will write your message, or you can employ a calligrapher. Incorporate your wedding theme and have it printed in your wedding colors by a local printer.

Sheaves of wheat. Symbolic of plenty and fruitfulness, wheat sheaves are a traditional gesture dating back to the Renaissance. Use them, with herbs, in lieu of bouquets or as decorations throughout your house, on the doors of your home or house of worship, and at the reception. These are particularly effective for a fall wedding.

Container herbs. Large pots of well-grown rosemary or other herbs can be recycled from a patio party, to showers, to line the steps into the church or synagogue, to the reception, and eventually to the newlyweds' first garden. Rosemary topiaries are particularly outstanding decorations. (Topiaries and herbs in large pots require working at least a year in advance or a cooperative greenhouse grower.)

Floating herbs. Cover squares of Styrofoam with flowers and herbs and float them in a garden pool for an outdoor summer wedding. As they drift freely, they will lend peace and beauty to the scene.

Cake knife. Tie a small bunch of herbs on the cake knife. Lily-of-the-valley (in silk, if it is out of season) can be included. Tie it with traditional narrow white ribbon streamers.

Picture frame. A "soft" frame made of satin, laces, and ribbons can be scented with a drop or two of essential oil.

The Wedding Ceremony

Invitations and announcements. Design your own invitations or announcements that include your wedding theme and colors and a sprig of pressed herbs. You can hand write them, and then have them printed on good card stock by your neighborhood printer.

Symbolism. If you write your own ceremony, or any part of it, mention your wedding herbs and flowers wherever appropriate. The quiet dignity of their symbolism will add a lovely and thoughtful touch.

Wedding program. Print the list of your chosen herbs and their symbolism in the wedding program, if you have one. You'll discover that most people save unusual programs such as these and will enjoy the sentiment expressed in your choice of herbs. It's also a grand opportunity for the happy couple to express

*She comes! Oh birds, to hail
    your queen combine,
With pipes and trills and
    wanderings mazy,
Singing — all Nature loves
    thee,
Queen White Daisy.*

— Thomas Hood,
nineteenth-century
English poet

THE BRIDE WAS SCENTSATIONAL!

You've planned this wedding for months. Do schedule a few relaxing hours for the most important person — the bride — and her personal needs. Enjoy a soothing bath with a favorite bath oil. This is a time to think only beautiful, unhurried thoughts. Wrap yourself in a big fluffy towel, and then begin "layering your fragrance" for a long and lasting aura. Use body lotions, followed by the sweet caress of perfumed talc. Spray cologne on your hair for a "veil of scent," and, while you are at it, scent an heirloom hanky to tuck in your sleeve. Saturate cotton balls with your favorite scent, stitch them on the hem of your petticoat, and know that you walk in beauty all during your unforgettable day.

their gratitude by extending a verbal "tussie-mussie" of accolades to all who helped with the herbs. (See pages 104–105.)

Ring bearer's pillow. Stuffed with fragrant dried herbs or potpourri, the ring bearer's pillow becomes a "scentimental" keepsake to enjoy forever as a bed pillow or tucked between your linens. If a moth mixture is used, one including lots of lavender blossoms, it can be packed away with the wedding gown, a traditional protective sachet as well as an heirloom keepsake. Personalize it with your monogram and the date, or use The Rosemary House's beautiful "Rosemary for Remembrance" sampler (see Mail-Order Sources on pages 181–182). If the pillow loses its fragrance, renew it with a few drops of your favorite essential oil. (See also pages 85–86.)

Photographs. Ask your photographer to include herbal vignettes among the wedding pictures to enhance your album of memories of this special day. Press some of the herbs so you can glue them between the photos ornamenting your treasured keepsake.

Rose petals. The British toss fresh rose petals at the

happy couple. If June is your wedding month and the rose garden is in full bloom, have a friend gather fully open roses the night before, pull the petals off and pop them into a plastic bag, then into the refrigerator. Add to your reminder list for the day — "Fill baskets (at the ready) with refrigerated rose petals and give to appointed young relatives to distribute to guests assembled after the wedding." **Note:** These are completely biodegradable. They curl up and disappear all on their own within a few hours of the wedding.

Kneeling bench. If your church uses a kneeling bench, devise a simple large rectangular herbal sachet for your wedding. Embroider it with your own and your fiancé's initials and the wedding date. As you kneel on the fragrant pillow, glorious aromas will be released into the air. Afterwards the flat pillow will serve as yet another keepsake, a sachet for your linen closet. (For sachets, see pages 80–84.)

Mints. My idea of heaven is to be wed at one of the 1,000-acre mint farms in the Midwest or Oregon — while it's being harvested. Oh, joy!

Flower girls. Have the flower girls carry baskets of fragrant potpourri, made well in advance, to strew (if allowed) or not, as you wish. Decorate a basket for wedding rice and the flower girls' baskets with bunches of herbs, fresh or dried, and ribbons in the wedding colors.

Guest book. Be sure to place a bouquet of fragrant herbs and flowers by the guest book. Tie a sprig of rosemary on the pen.

Flowers

Wedding bouquet. Have your herbal bridal bouquet photographed professionally close up. Then, as they did in Victorian days, commission an artist to paint it on canvas and frame it for posterity. Insert small prints of the photograph in your thank-you notes for one last romantic souvenir.

Flowers from the wedding service. Herbal bouquets used in the house of worship can do double duty as centerpieces at the wedding reception. Put the groomsmen in charge of transporting the bouquets after the official photographs are taken.

"Please pass the smelling salts!"

Guests

If she's from Long Island and he's from San Diego, assist wedding guests in finding housing and entertainment before and after the ceremony. Your special day could prove to be their long weekend. Fragrant bunches of herbs should welcome them in their rooms upon arrival, along with a greeting on herbal notepaper listing the schedule of events, things to do in the area, perhaps an invitation to a brunch buffet on Saturday or Sunday, special places to visit (local herb gardens!), and useful phone numbers. It's a good idea to enlist the aid of willing friends and other family members living in the area. Remember, memories are made by extra little herbal touches.

Keeping Calm in the Midst of It All: Aromatherapy

I'm convinced we make so much ado about weddings because of the importance of such an event in our lives. It ranks with birth and death, events over which one has little control. The emotional buildup equates to wear and tear on the nerves. This nervous energy in turn fuels the wedding preparation activity that mounts with the proximity to the date. Nerves and stress become synonymous — a truism that has always been so. Herbs to the rescue!

To counteract the stress of accelerating wedding preparations, and indeed the wedding day itself, surround yourself

AROMATHERAPY OILS	EFFECT
Lavender, rose, jasmine	To relax
Peppermint, rose, lemon	To excite the spirits
Peppermint, spearmint, rosemary	To clear the head
Rosewood, rose geranium, basil, pine	To stimulate
Rosemary, juniper, eucalyptus	To erase aches and pains

— and everyone involved — with fragrances. The technique of using herbs to relieve nerves and stress is known as *aromatherapy*. Books have been written on the subject, and great universities have researched the effectiveness of fragrance and herbs. The calming influence of herbs cannot be denied.

Try it for yourself. Herbs can quiet the nerves and temper emotions as needed. Breathe deeply and enjoy fragrances that please you. Drink herbal teas while engaged in the seemingly endless wedding projects and preparations. And treat yourself to many relaxing herbal baths. They work wonders.

Herbs for the Bath

Combine the dried herbs, and store them in a clear glass jar. They are decorative as well as useful. Simmer 1 cupful in 1 quart water for 5 minutes. Strain into your bath water, and relax. Think only about what you have already crossed off your list of things to be done.

1 cup dried mint

1 cup dried rosemary

1 cup dried lavender flowers

1 cup dried rose petals

1 cup dried comfrey leaves (optional)

1 cup dried lovage

LOVE BATH BALLS

1. Cut 4-inch squares of heart-print fabric.

2. Place 1 teaspoon of *Herbs for the Bath* mixture in the center of the fabric.

3. Draw up the four corners, and tie tightly into a sachet using a 10-inch length of wool yarn. Each ball makes one relaxing bath.

Wedding Parties of All Kinds

$\mathbf{A}$LWAYS FESTIVE, prenuptial parties are the get-to-gether family and friends enjoy most. Don't hesitate to festoon these galas liberally with herbs in every possible way.

The Announcement

The occasion for a betrothed couple to make their family and friends aware of their future plans can be a large social gathering, a tea party, a luncheon with "the girls," or a simple announcement of intentions.

The engagement ring is now often the first evidence of the betrothal promise, but you may want to offer a simple announcement as well. Rosemary — "that's for remembrance" — can be part of a lovely symbolic gesture. Distribute little sprigs of the herb tied with ribbons and a small white card with your own and your fiancé's name and your wedding date. It's a singular way to reserve the wedding day on busy calen-

A little garden in which to
   walk,
an immensity in which to
   dream,
at one's feet that which can
   be cultivated and plucked;
overhead that which one can
   study and meditate upon;
some herbs on earth and all
   the stars in the sky.

        — Victor Hugo

dars. If rosemary plants are not available or not of sufficient size to supply many sprigs, attach to the card tiny packets of whole dried rosemary from your spice cupboard.

You can also use myrtle, which has been symbolic of love and the emblem of marriage for centuries. If available, hand out little sprigs of fragrant myrtle, the true *Myrtus communis* of Biblical times, tied with small white bows and attached to your printed or handwritten engagement message. If you wish to send an announcement note to distant friends and relatives, your rosemary or myrtle sprig travels well in the mail.

If you want people to join in your festivities, adapt any of the party suggestions in this book, and use the herbs and recipes in part II. If you are in an office or school, belong to a big family, or participate in the activities of a rather good-sized congregation, you might consider setting your herbal theme right at the start. Place a tray of heart-shaped herb cookies decorated with the initials of both you and your fiancé and a small standing announcement in a prominent spot — it will provide the excitement for that day. Because caraway seeds were once given to engaged couples to keep them from straying — caraway is said to confer the "gift of retention" — it might be fun to use the recipe for *Crisp Caraway Cookies* in chapter 9 (page 140).

For more elaborate parties, include herbs in the invitation, as favors, as centerpieces to decorate the food table, in corsages for the mothers of the bride- and groom-to-be, and in the menu, especially in the herbal punch. Be prepared to distribute copies of the recipes to all in attendance, because they will be intrigued by your herbal refreshments. Perhaps these can be favors, again repeating the names of the happy couple and the date of the wedding to come.

Continuing the Festivities

From this happy beginning until the wedding itself, many opportunities for honoring the future bride or groom or both will arise. Here are more suggestions for teas, picnics, dinner parties, showers, and other ways to entertain — with herbs!

A British Tea

A summertime tea, British style, can be as formal or informal as you wish. On one occasion we created an oversized table by setting boards on sawhorses on our freshly swept and reorganized side porch. With the table dressed with a queen-sized lavender sheet topped with our best polyester lace, our old porch had never looked so festive. A bouffant bouquet of wedding-like Queen-Anne's-lace from a nearby field was surrounded by low bowls filled with small tussie-mussies, a myriad of extremely casual bunches tied with colorful bows. These were our favors for all attending, both ladies and gentlemen. (Instructions for making tussie-mussies are on pages 37–41.)

At one end of our long table were beribboned baskets of English lavender sachets, additional souvenirs for guests. At the opposite end of the table was a large punch bowl, filled with *Royal Wedding Punch* afloat with garnishes of herbs and flowers. One gentleman savored his, sipping and sniffing it like fine wine. Along with the punch, we served *Rose Petal Sandwiches*, *Lemon Balm Jelly* on tiny salted crackers, and little *Herbwiches*. *Candied Violets* and other herbal sweetmeats made popular nibblers. (Recipes can be found in part II.)

A Herbal Bridal Party Alfresco

To announce the wedding, shower the bride, or greet the newly married couple, entertain outdoors, weather permitting. Everyone loves a picnic, so why not? But, make this a picnic with a difference — serve an elegant menu *à la herbs*.

Select burlap cloths and pottery, checkered tablecloths and paper plates, or no-iron terry cloth and Melamine — or go all out and use linen and china. Remember, there are no laws. Array the center of the tables with a large number of matched green mineral water bottles. Gather an assortment of gay garden flowers and herbs, and place one or two in each bottle. Intersperse these with your "favorite things." What centerpiece could be easier, more effective, or as charming?

Give each guest a palm-leaf fan, with a bunch of basil and lemon balm attached by a pretty ribbon. As guests fan themselves, the herbs will scent the warm air, while at the same time keep away flies and gnats — important at a picnic.

When it is time for your guests to move toward the picnic area, give each one a hobo stick with eating utensils and soft dinner rolls filled with shrimp salad wrapped in a colorful work handkerchief.

To go with this, consider this beautiful, delicious, and well-herbed menu: *Katy's Blueberry Soup, Salad à Fleur, Dip with Crudités, Fruit Skewers,* and *Iced Herb Tea* (see part II for recipes).

Matching favors could be little hobo stick (pipe cleaners or small twigs) sachets.

Place shrimp salad sandwiches and eating utensils on a colorful handkerchief and knot to a stick, hobo-style. Create small matching sachets to offer as party favors.

A Progressive Dinner Party

In a close-knit family or extremely compatible neighborhood, a travelling party is a fun way to entertain. Each course — from soup to nuts — is served at a different house, each host and hostess featuring a different herb, decor, dish, or favor.

This party can travel between three houses or twelve, depending upon your inspiration, cooperation, and enthusiasm. One impromptu committee meeting should divide the work evenly, so that everyone enjoys the party.

Write up the recipes and package dried herbs used at each party stop to present them to the bride- and groom-to-be along with the dessert. Other gifts from guests can be table centerpieces, to be opened at each stop as the party progresses.

A Herbal Kitchen Shower

Use herbs in abundance and a pretty color scheme, too. Don't forget to include some of your own favorite things — baskets, a doll collection, antiques, or an assortment of hearts. Here are some other ideas to help set the stage.

Invitations. Glue pressed herbs or dried spices onto handwritten or purchased invitations. Ask each person to bring along a favorite recipe and the main seasoning ingredient to go with it, and then give the bride-to-be a recipe file, a spice cupboard, or an attractive basket to receive these special personalized herbal goodies.

Centerpiece. In the center of the table or buffet, group many "things herbal," such as pots or bunches of herbs, dried herbs in apothecary jars, a cookbook, glass jars or bowls of colorful potpourri, scented candles, a mortar and pestle, whole spices, and a kitchen towel with herbs on it. These can make a charming grouping, like a photo on the cover of your favorite herbal, especially when placed on a wooden board or in a flat basket. They can be from the hostess's collection or additional herbal gifts for the honored guests.

Another idea for a centerpiece is an adaptation of fragrant "spice posies," a souvenir from a little shop in Austria. Bits of whole cloves, cinnamon, allspice, ginger, and nutmeg are glued onto a lacy white paper doily to be hung over the stove where the steamy heat of cooking releases their spicy fragrance. The posy could also be kept under a glass dome in the living room, opened to sniff and closed to keep it pretty and fragrant and clean. Spices, dried golden yarrow, glue, doilies, and ribbons are all you need to make these delightful Old

*Make a "spice posy" by gluing assorted spices
into a flat head of golden yarrow, backed by
a white paper doily and using the yarrow
stem as a "handle".*

World charmers. It's easy to glue the whole spices into the golden heads of yarrow, an herb for "a love that lasts." Use a cluster of them as the centerpiece, and then distribute them as favors.

Gifts. Suggest that guests bring such gifts as kitchen gadgets, herbal things, or whatever the bride needs. A spice trousseau (see page 28) is a nice idea.

Favors. Any of the following simple gifts would make a lovely favor.

♥ Herb charts rolled into a scroll with a bag of parsley, sage, rosemary, or thyme, and tied with a bow in your color scheme.

♥ A recipe served at the party, written on a card with a tablespoon of the main seasoning ingredient attached in a small envelope.

♥ A nosegay of fresh herbs with symbolism attached — marjoram for joy, thyme for courage, rosemary for remembrance, and so on — all tied with ribbons and laces.

♥ A small bottle of your favorite seasoned salt, herb jelly, or homemade tarragon vinegar for each guest.

♥ A packet of herb seeds to grow in one's own garden is always popular, especially if it is a gift from your garden to theirs. (Be sure the bride-to-be receives a packet of each kind you distribute.)

♥ Little pots of herbs, labeled, which can be used in the center of the table as decoration, too.

♥ An old-fashioned nutmeg grater and nutmeg tied with ribbons in the party colors.

♥ A whole long cinnamon stick with the recipe for *Hot Mulled Cider* attached (see chapter 12).

♥ Small sacks or sachets of wedding rice (see pages 88–90) — rice with rosemary "for remembrance" and roses "for love" — to be used at the wedding.

♥ Plastic bathroom tiles heated in a 280°F oven until soft and pliable, and shaped over a flat-bottomed object to create a holder for little herb bouquets, a bit of potpourri, or mints.

♥ A cored large green pear or bright red apple, filled with a bunch of parsley, herbs, and tiny flowers. One at each place is quite effective.

Menu. Advance planning is the secret. Have herbal sandwiches, an herbal dip, spicy cake or cookies, and edible flowers, too, as a garnish or to eat. There are so many good things to serve that include herbs and spices. By all means, serve a good herb tea — peppermint, rose hip, camomile, whatever you think your guests will enjoy, hot or cold, iced or spiced. Homemade herb tea or Bigelow's Constant Comment tea is always a hit at a party. It's fun, too, to put an attractive basket of assorted herb tea bags on the party tea tray. Some guests will try more than one kind.

Extras. Do use herbal napkins. Be sure to garnish the food liberally with herbs and colorful edible flowers (unsprayed). Bouquets of fragrant herbs throughout the house, especially in the powder room, and a dried herbal wreath on the door add charming ambience. Greet the guest of honor with a herbal tussie-mussie (see pages 37–41).

Herbs Say the Nicest Things for Anniversaries

Let's not overlook anniversaries as occasions for parties. The years pile up. Before you know it, your first anniversary will be here — with many others to follow. It is inevitable.

Once again, the herbal ideas for menus, punch bowls, gifts, favors, and decorations abound. There are traditional anniversary symbols as well as a few more recent tokens to consider. Select your theme and color scheme from this

WEDDING ANNIVERSARIES

YEAR	TRADITIONAL	CONTEMPORARY
First	Paper	Wine/Flowers
Second	Cotton	Books
Third	Leather	Houseplants
Fourth	Flowers	Pottery
Fifth	Wood	Crystal/Glass
Sixth	Candy	Copper
Seventh	Wool	Linens
Eighth	Bronze	Wood
Ninth	Pottery	Pewter
Tenth	Tin	Art
Eleventh	Steel	Gourmet cookware
Twelfth	Silk	Leather
Thirteenth	Lace	Clocks/Watches
Fourteenth	Ivory	Iron
Fifteenth	Crystal	Pearls
Twentieth	China	China
Twenty-fifth	Silver	Silver
Thirtieth	Pearl	Coral
Thirty-fifth	Coral	Jade
Fortieth	Ruby	Ruby
Forty-fifth	Sapphire	Sapphire
Fiftieth	Gold	Gold
Fifty-fifth	Emerald	Emerald
Sixtieth	Diamond	Diamond
Seventy-fifth	Diamond	Diamond

accepted list and start planning the party. From the paper anniversary to the diamond, herbs lend themselves to all celebrations. Their enchantment will linger long after the party ends — until the next anniversary.

Gifting the Bride and Groom

Prewedding parties and the wedding itself offer many opportunities for gift giving. Herb-loving brides and grooms will be especially touched if the gifts they receive include these special plants.

A Herb and Spice Trousseau

Anise	Curry powder	Nutmeg (whole, with a grater)	Sesame seed
Basil	Dill (seed and weed)	Onion (powder, salt, and flakes)	Sage (rubbed)
Bay leaves (whole and/or ground)	Fennel (whole)	Oregano	Seasoned salt(s)
Cayenne pepper	Garlic (powder, chips, or salt)	Parsley	Soy sauce
Chile powder	Ginger (ground)	Paprika	Tabasco sauce
Cinnamon (sticks and ground)	Marjoram	Pepper (preferably whole, with a grinder)	Tarragon
Cloves (whole and ground)	Mint	Poppyseed	Worcestershire sauce
	Mustard powder		

This list can go on and on, ad infinitum, but it's a beginning. Cardamom, saffron, juniper berries, and cilantro can be added later. It might be fun to throw a herb-and-spice shower where friends contribute the necessities to fill a handsome cabinet with tried-and-true recipes or cookbooks to get the couple off on the right track.

The Newlyweds' Herb and Spice Cabinet

To stock a proper seasoning shelf, gather together the herbs and spices listed in the box above — and others, if you wish — either fresh and dried from the garden (the best) or purchased in matched bottles. These will represent a good-sized investment. To preserve the flavor, be sure they are stored away from heat, light, and humidity. A herb-and-spice chart would go well with this trousseau of seasonings.

Their New Herb Garden — For Now and Forever

My favorite wedding gift is a door decoration — a broom-corn whisk broom tied with a bunch of fresh or dried herbs, lots of bows, and a few crisp twenty-dollar bills caught in the ribbons. The card to the newlyweds reads "For Mr. and Mrs. _____'s New Herb Garden."

There is no greater joy than planning and planting, tending and harvesting a brand new little herb garden. Whether

Plants for a small herb garden would be a treasured gift: (clockwise from top) bee balm, mint, sage, chives, parsley, basil.

it be a few windowsill containers, a tub outside the condo door, or a plot in a sunny spot close to the most-used entrance, I always like to encourage another new herb patch. Easy to grow, these gardens offer tremendous rewards.

A small city backyard lends itself to herb gardening; patterned paths and divided areas can give a minuscule space the feel of a well-planned estate. There is no doubt that even from a very small space, herbs have the largest harvest, most pleasant and useful, of anything you plant and tend.

Apartment herb gardening is possible in a sunny south window or, sometimes better, under grow lights on the kitchen counter. Matched pots of pretty herbs can yield an unexpected amount of herbal pleasure. Keep cutting scissors handy!

If the bride and groom are not already gardeners, perhaps the herb garden gift money could be tied onto a good basic how-to-grow-and-use-them herbal.

Brave brides once carried herb plants, seeds, or divisions as precious cargo in saddlebags or covered wagons. It is time-honored tradition dating back to the *Mayflower*, when packets of herb seeds were brought to new homes to be nurtured, treasured, and used through the years. As in days of old, the gardens that supply the wedding herbs can be counted upon to provide some starts for the newest herb garden. When the couple moves on to their second home, they can take along small plants. A few herbs, treasured mementos from their honeymoon haven, are easily transferred to another garden plot.

Framed Announcement

A treasured wedding announcement or invitation preserved in a gold shadow box and surrounded with symbolic herbs and flowers is the best of all possible gifts to a bride and groom — or to yourselves. See pages 76–77 for instructions.

CHAPTER 3

Flowers and Herbs for Your Wedding

THE ELOQUENCE OF HERBS is never more apparent than in a bridal bouquet. They speak of many things — of ancient wisdom and future joy. The three most important wedding herbs are myrtle, orange blossom, and rosemary (of course!). These three have been used for centuries to decorate wedding halls, to fashion garlands and crowns, and to enhance bridal bouquets.

The Romans crowned their brides with myrtle, a delightfully fragrant small-leafed evergreen shrub. True *Myrtus communis* is not the creeping ground cover we call myrtle today. Throughout what is now Eastern Europe, far back in antiquity, this true myrtle is revered as a symbol of wedded bliss. The ancient Egyptians, Hebrews, Romans, and Greeks recorded the virtues of this fragrant, almost sacred, herb and always in association with love and marriage. Emblem of "divine generosity," sprigs of true myrtle are still worn tradition-

Take thou this rose,
O rose
Since love's own flower it
is,
And by that rose
That lover captive is.

— Anonymous
Renaissance troubadour

Myrtle

Orange blossoms

ally by both bride and groom in many European countries, a carryover from those Roman days. The maid-of-honor took home a sprig of the bridal crown of myrtle, which she was expected to root as a symbol of her own future love and happiness, perhaps to be worn in her own wedding crown.

Orange blossoms are still coveted by today's bride with traditional leanings. The waxen white blossoms with their overpowering fragrance are symbolic of joy, happiness, and fecundity. Scent and sentiment abound for brides wearing orange blossoms. Because orange blossoms are sometimes hard to get in northern areas, the equally fragrant white blossoms of the Ponderosa lemon tree (*Citrus limon* 'Ponderosa'), a houseplant, make a good substitute.

Rosemary speaks also of joy and good wishes in a bridal bouquet. Shakespeare referred to the charming wedding party custom of distributing sprigs of gilded rosemary tied with ribbons called "bride's laces." For more on the customs associated with rosemary, see pages 5–6.

We have perhaps overlooked these "loving herbs" because they are greenhouse plants in northern climates and not always easy to find. "Second-day air" may make it possible today (see Mail-Order Sources on pages 181–182). All may be grown as houseplants and summered outdoors. Indeed, they are quite satisfactory as container plants if supplied with a sunny window, cool room, good soil, and occasional misting with water. Dried myrtle leaves and rosemary, however, as well as orange blossom oil, are always available.

Conditioning Is Crucial

The single most important step in preparing flowers and herbs for any party, especially a wedding, is cutting and conditioning them properly. Take time to condition your herbs and flowers to avoid the embarrassment of wilted bouquets. Hanging flower heads and drooping herbs can be depressing, but if you prepare them properly, they will hold well.

Conditioning (sometimes called *hardening*) means fill-

As with other bridal fashions, there have always been cycles during which various bridal flowers have been favored. Since the orange blossom has enjoyed a full century of popularity, however, it is interesting to know something about this delicate, beautiful flower.

Carried from Spain to America on Columbus's second voyage, the orange tree is one of the wonders of nature, as it bears fruits and flowers all year long and at the same time. Because of this, the orange blossom has come to symbolize the young and fruitful bride.

The incredibly sweet fragrance of orange blossoms can be overpowering. The essential oil (called neroli) is perfect for bridal potpourri. The tradition of using orange blossoms is so much a part of weddings that sometimes wax flowers are used when fresh blossoms are unobtainable.

ing the stems with water until they become turgid, or hard. This process gives your plant material a chance to recover from the trauma of being severed from its lifeline — the roots — and provides the necessary water and stamina so that stressed cuttings will serve you a long time.

Florist flowers come to you direct from refrigeration. Even so, it will pay you dividends if you recut their stems on a slant and plunge them into fresh, cool water containing a commercial conditioner. Keep them cool, dark, and draft-free until required.

Commercial conditioners are convenient and worth their modest cost. Using them is a good way to secure your investment of time, money, and energy, as well as to ensure that flowers and herbs last through the ceremony with or without additional moisture. (Do not use commercial conditioners if the herbs are likely to be eaten.)

Because wildflowers and herbs are by nature thirsty, they need to be given special attention from the moment they are gathered. To prevent wilting, carry a bucket of warm water (80° to 100°F) with conditioner added, directly to the field or garden. Use a very sharp knife or pruner to cut stems on a long slant (this offers a greater area for water absorption). Remove all lower leaves, lest they decay underwater, and promptly place the stems in deep water. As soon as possible, get the buckets into a cool, dark, draft-free place for at least eight hours of conditioning. Under refrigeration, if at all possible, some materials will last several weeks. Covering your gatherings loosely with lightweight plastic provides additional protection. In hot weather, I place buckets of ice under the plastic covers along with the buckets full of flowers.

This may seem like a lot of work, perhaps even unnecessary, but it is essential to the success of your project. Trust me!

For long-lasting bouquets, proper conditioning is essential. Cut stems at a sharp angle, remove lower leaves, and plunge immediately into a bucket of warm water. Keep cool for at least eight hours before arranging.

FLORAL MECHANICS

Water-absorbing floral foam comes in many useful forms, including wreaths; blocks; posy holders; stick-ons for doors, walls, and mirrors; candlestick adapters; pew bouquet holders; and more. Your local craft shop or florist can assist you in finding these undeniably useful products, all of which lend themselves to herbal wedding work. They are designed to make floral arrangements of all kinds ridiculously easy. Just soak the compact and versatile foam. Once it is filled with water, you can insert short, well-conditioned sprigs of herbs and flowers. Cut all stems an equal length for a well-rounded bouquet.

Here are a few tips from experts:

♥ A tried-and-true formula for keeping finished arrangements fresh is 1 can water to 1 can 7-Up or Sprite and H teaspoon bleach.

♥ Group together small, fragile flowers or herbs (such as violets or thyme), and tie them together in bunches. Condition these delicate materials in suitable small-sized containers.

♥ Remember that petals and foliage absorb as much water as roots and stems. Keep a mister of water handy, and use it freely.

♥ Most herbs are much easier to condition in fall than in spring, when in their youthful exuberance they grow too fast. To convert soft growth into hardened stems, you may have to condition the tender foliage twice in spring. Recut the thirsty stems, and put them back in warm water. Use only those that are turgid.

♥ Cut your flowers and herbs very early in the morning or after the heat of the sun leaves the day. Plants are at their peak and contain the most sugar during cool mornings and evenings.

♥ To preserve homegrown roses or tulips that are in danger of opening or shattering before the occasion, dip the blossoms into a glue of frothy egg white. Remove the excess as you press the flower into shape. Not only is this treatment invisible, but the flowers will never open further.

Herbal Wedding Bouquets

A simple bunch of herbs and flowers can be carried as is, formed into a circular posy (tussie-mussie), or arranged in a basket for an informal wedding.

You can arrange the bouquet yourself or find a cooperative florist who will work the herbs into the wedding flowers for you. See to it that the florist has them in plenty of time before the wedding, so that the herbs can be well integrated into the overall plan. Here are a half dozen or so ideas for bridal bouquets.

Herb Bouquet on a Hoop

This is pretty and easy to do. Purchase a 14-inch wooden hoop from a craft shop that carries macramé supplies. Wrap the hoop with white satin ribbon, beginning and ending with transparent tape. At the tape, securely fasten an informal bouquet of herbs with or without other flowers. It may need to be tied on twice, so that it doesn't slip. Both the bride and bridesmaids can carry it over the rim, in front, with herbs at the top or the bottom of the hoop. Ribbon streamers are optional. The nice part about these bouquets is that they can be used during the reception as decorations. Determine in advance an effective place to hang them.

A satin-covered hoop, garnished with an informal bouquet of herbs and flowers makes a lovely, easy-to-do bridesmaid's bouquet.

Nosegays All Around

Herbal nosegays, or tussie-mussies, can be carried by the bride, her attendants, all the mothers, and honored guests. You may even wish to offer miniature ones to every guest attending. If you have a large garden and a sizeable group of friends, these old-fashioned favorites can be whipped up in no time for a memorable wedding. There are several ways to make tussie-mussies. I describe a more elaborate one first, followed by a simpler technique. In either case, for the herb sprigs, use lemon balm, mints, rosemary, myrtle, sage, parsley, thyme, rue (not in hot weather), marjoram, oregano, lavenders, lemon geranium, southernwood, yarrow, and tansy in an assortment of shapes, textures, and fragrances, and in soft gray, green, and golden hues. For the ribbon, assorted narrow widths are always lovely. The accompanying instructions make one bride's bouquet.

1 bouquet holder

1 lace-edged collar for the bouquet holder

White florist's tape

5 yards double-faced white satin ribbons

6 mini-carnations (or roses or daisies)

One 8-inch piece #26 wire

A variety of herb sprigs, approximately 5 to 6 inches long

6 larger leaves (scented geraniums, sage, variegated bishop's weed, or ivy)

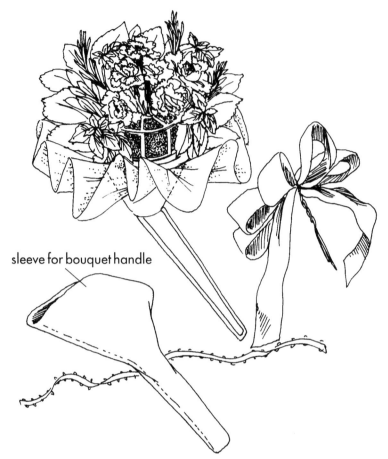

sleeve for bouquet handle

Bridal nosegays are made by arranging short stems of herbs and flowers in a purchased bouquet holder.

1. Make your bow (see pages 66), and secure it with wire to use as a stem for easy insertion when the tussie-mussie is completed. Set it aside.

2. Wet the floral foam in the bouquet holder and slide the lacy collar onto the holder.

3. Tape the plastic handle, securing the lace collar by its "tails," or purchase a satin sleeve to cover the handle.

4. Place the herbs gently but firmly into the damp foam. Angle them slightly as you work, so they fall gracefully into place. Start in the center and work toward the outside. Place the largest leaves around the perimeter to form a decorative collar around the base. If you have two of any herb, balance them by placing them opposite each other. If you have three sprigs, place them equidistant in triangle formation. Place four matched pieces N, E, S, and W, compass-style. Poke in five stems in a star pattern. Proceed in this manner, always working in balance.

5. Place the central flower — a carnation or rose. Surround it carefully with your other flowers, in balance. Tuck in baby's-breath, if you wish.

6. Mist the bouquet, swathe it in plastic, and refrigerate it until just before the ceremony.

7. Insert the wired bow where it is best displayed.

SIMPLICITY PERSONIFIED

You may carry a single long-stemmed rose with a sprig of rosemary, if you so desire. In this case, "less is more" and most impressive.

Even in severe climates, you can gather certain hardy herb tips — thyme, winter savory, sage, rue, lavender, southernwood, burnet, hyssop. Toss them into a bucket of warm water, saying, "Wake up!" and they will spring back to life. Combine with rosemary and myrtle from the windowsill and a few florist flowers — say, "roses for love" — to make a traditional circular nosegay. Add laces and ribbons, if you wish.

An alternate method for making tussie-mussies is suitable when you are making quantities of nosegays. Except when I make the bride's bouquet, I almost always make nosegays "in hand," without benefit of a florist's holder. These circular nosegays are also popular for proms, anniversaries, and many other occasions, as well as for weddings. (See color photo, page 91) Use white or colored flowers and one or more different kinds of herbs — all rosemary, if you like, or a mixture of herbs chosen for their symbolism or their availability. Net, bows, streamers, lace, and doilies are all optional, in white or assorted colors, as you like. Cover stems with foil or, for more elegance, florist's tape covered with velvet ribbon secured with straight pins. In addition to the herbs and flowers, you will require raffia or a spool of linen florist's thread.

Hold and start with the central flower, preferably a rosebud on a 6- to 8-inch stem, dethorned. Carefully place all the well-conditioned herbs (see pages 32–36) around it in concentric circles of foliage, along with additional flowers from your garden, or purchased.

Place a fringe of thyme or curled parsley around the central bud. Keep turning your nosegay as you build it, until it is as large and full as you wish. Distribute all other herbs as described in step 4 in "Nosegays All Around" (page 39), carefully balanced in hand. As you add surrounding layers, wrap the stems with soft thread, raffia, or florist's tape to bind them together. Use the largest leaves for the outermost collar of herbs.

Surround the herbs and flowers with a ruffle of lace, if desired. Ruffle the lace by stringing it on an 8-inch piece of wire, and collar it around the nosegay, open end at the bow.

Because this bouquet has no source of water, mist it well and refrigerate it to ensure its survival. At the last minute, add the bow and either tape or foil the stem mass. After the wedding, remove the foil, and place the bouquet in a goblet of water, where all can enjoy its beauty, charm, and fragrance for a week or so.

When constructing a nosegay without using a bouquet holder, begin with the central flower and work outward, adding herbs and flowers in concentric circles. Tape stems and surround nosegay with a lace ruffle.

TUSSIE-MUSSIES

Tussie-mussies go back to Medieval times. These bouquets of sweet-smelling herbs were carried by ladies to protect them from bad air. More recently, Queen Elizabeth II was presented with one at her coronation in Westminster Abbey, as a symbol of her high rank.

Tussie-mussies include fragrant herbs as well as symbolic herbs, such as:

Roses for Love • Artemisia for Constancy • Mint for Joy • Lavender for Luck • Sage for Good Health • Thyme for Courage • Lemon Balm for Comfort • Rosemary for Remembrance

If it has stems, you may keep your tussie-mussie fresh for a week in water, and then allow it to dry to last forever.

Tussie-mussies, fresh or dried, large or small, formal rounds or simple bunches, are especially appropriate for an herbal wedding. Present them to guests with an explanation of the meanings of the herbs and their care.

Fill a plastic-lined basket with moist floral foam, then arrange herbs and flowers as desired, beginning with the most plentiful plant material.

Basket of Herbs

Choose the basket carefully. Practice carrying it about to see if it is comfortable to carry. Line it with plastic, and then stuff it with well-saturated floral foam. Poke the short stems of well-conditioned herbs into the foam until the basket is filled. Use the herb you have the most of first, and fill in with the others as you go along. Flowers may be included, of course, and bows are always pretty. Work with stems of the same length. Remember, there's always room for "just one more."

Sometimes I tuck in at the center a small bunch of the herbs, tied separately, to be removed and thrown at the end of the reception party. Be sure the herbs are well secured, if you think the bride will toss them vigorously.

Herbs for a Bible or Prayer Book

Gather about two dozen sprigs of herbs. Divide them into two groups, and cover each group of stems with florist's tape. Place one bunch up and the other down, and tie them together in the middle using narrow white satin bridal ribbons. Attach streamers. Keep this herbal delight in plastic under refrigeration until you are ready to attach it to your Bible or prayer book. If it is to become a family heirloom, take a photograph of it, and paste it inside the book for posterity.

Fasten two bouquets together, end to end, and attach them to a Bible or prayer book.

Wedding Mats

These are gay and unusual — attendants will love them. Take a flat wicker mat, and weave ribbons through the outer openings, leaving streamers at the bottom. Attach a pipe cleaner handle to the back. Fasten two bouquets together, end to end, as described in "Herbs for a Bible or Prayer Book," and attach them to the center of the mats. Tuck in some dried rosebuds along with other pods and herbs that dry well, such as yarrow, knotted marjoram, lunaria (silver dollars), lavender, or baby's-breath. After the wedding is over, bridesmaids can use these as lovely wall hangings.

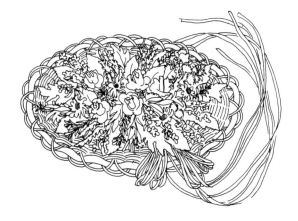

Fasten together two small bouquets of herbs and flowers, end to end, and attach to a ribbon-decorated wicker mat.

6 long-stemmed red roses
(for love)

1 long stem sage (for health
and domestic tranquility)

1 long stem rosemary (for
remembrance)

1 long stem mint (for joy)

1 long stem lavender (for
luck)

1 long stem yarrow (for a
love that's long and true)

1 long stem myrtle (traditional symbol of love)

1 long stem southernwood
(for fun and fragrance)

1 yard #3 or #9 red velvet
ribbon

The soul of simplicity, this easiest-to-assemble arrangement (no wire, no tape) is the most sophisticated bride's bouquet. It has the coveted bare-stem, fresh-from-the-garden, casual look. (For color photo, see page 96.

Cut each herb and flower stem at least 12 inches long, and condition the materials very well (see pages 32–36).

Remove all thorns and foliage on the lower half of the stems of roses and herbs. Assemble a hand-held bouquet by taking up a rose, a herb, a rose, a herb, and so on, until you have used everything in a simple clutch of slightly crossing stems. Wire all together where the stems meet. Cover the wire by tieing a simple shoelace-type bow with streamers. Tie the knots. Done!

Note: Since this bouquet has no source of water and the stems are exposed, unprotected by tape, it must be kept in a Styrofoam cooler until needed. If you make slightly smaller ones for each bridesmaid, keep each one in its own cooler. Keep them misted and dewy fresh.

A simple, but sophisticated, bare-stem bouquet is made by alternating long-stemmed roses and herbs and fastening them with wire and ribbon.

Use a purchased bouquet holder to create a cascade-style bridal bouquet.

Cascade Bouquet

Here is the traditional cascade-style bridal bouquet with a difference — herbs! Although fresh herbs are available from the herb garden during most of the year or by mail (see Mail-Order Sources on pages 181–182), you may substitute other herbs for those listed below, if necessary. Remember, everything that is cut for use needs to be well conditioned (see pages 32–36). If you can provide the herbs, a florist can create this traditional bridal bouquet.

1. Wet the floral foam thoroughly.

2. Attach the lace collar firmly by pushing the holder stem through the center opening.

3. Tape the bouquet holder handle with white florist's tape. Be sure to secure the lace collar. (**Optional:** Wrap the taped plastic holder stem with ribbon to match the bow. Secure with a straight pin.)

1 bouquet holder with floral foam

One 10-inch lace-edged form for bouquet holder

White florist's tape

5 yards #3 ribbon for a bow (optional; see pages 65–66)

Small piece of wire

6 large lamb's-ears leaves

4 large scented geranium leaves

5 sprays small-leafed ivy (1 long, 2 medium, 2 short)

9 stems roses in bride's choice of color

4 pieces myrtle

4 sprigs sage

10 stems lavender

10 stems thyme

5 stems rosemary

5 cuttings of rue (in hot weather substitute southernwood)

3 stems mint

3 sprigs lemon balm (or lemon verbena or lemon geranium)

Baby's-breath (optional)

4. Make your bow and hold it together with a piece of wire, which becomes its stem. Set aside.

5. Arrange the lamb's-ears symmetrically around the perimeter, pushing the stems into the wetted foam.

6. Intersperse geranium leaves between the lamb's-ears. Gently but firmly push stems into the foam.

7. Carefully place ivy stems in a cascade at the bottom, with the longest one centered and two on each side in a V formation. Bear in mind the height of the bride when measuring the length of the ivy.

8. Place roses or other flowers of choice as shown, centered and cascading. Cut each stem a different length to achieve a staggered cascade.

9. Fill in completely with additional herbal foliage. Cut the sprigs different lengths and balance the placement. For example, place one on each side, three in a sort of triangle, one in each quarter, and so on.

10. If you use it, place the baby's-breath last, here and there throughout.

11. If you use a bow, arrange it at one side of the bottom and allow the cascading streamers to mingle with the ivy.

An Elegant Crescent Bouquet

1. Fold the ribbon in half, then fold the 2-yard lengths in half again and once again to make ½-yard loops. Twist a wire around the center of the cascade of loops. Set the bow aside.

2. Wet the floral foam.

3. Slide the lace collar onto the bouquet holder.

4. Tape the handle, securing the collar by its plastic "fringe."

5. Place the herbal foliage and ivy first, cascading the long ivy on either side of the holder to form the crescent. Fill in with the fragrant herbs. Use longer stems to help form the classic crescent; center the larger leafed herbs.

6. Cut the rose stems to graduated lengths and place them throughout the crescent, six on each side.

4 yards #2 satin ribbon

Small piece of wire

1 bouquet holder with floral foam

One 10-inch bouquet collar, ivory or white lace

White florist's tape

5 large herb leaves (for example, 'Mabel Gray' geraniums)

12 assorted lengths small-leafed ivy (from 5 to 12 inches)

24 assorted herb sprigs (from 5 to 10 inches), rosemary, myrtle, sage, rue, mints, lemon balm, verbena, lavenders, marjoram, southernwood

12 roses

3 lilies

6 small calla lilies (or carnations)

This formal bouquet is created on a foam-filled purchased holder, with lilies at the center surrounded by herbs and roses, from which ivy cascades in graceful arcs.

7. Cut the lily stems as short as necessary (about 4 to 5 inches) and center them in the arrangement.

8. Cut the calla (or carnation or garden flower) stems in graduated lengths to reinforce the crescent, and use them to fill in between the roses and herbs.

9. Keep the bouquet misted, covered with plastic, and refrigerated until the last minute — a plastic cooler with ice will do. Plunge the wired bow into the bottom center of the crescent in front of the handle.

Herbal Heart Bouquet

2 #20-gauge 18-inch wires

White or green florist's tape

Assorted herb sprigs (3 to 5 inches)

Assorted flower buds (3 to 5 inches)

4 yards narrow white velvet ribbon

A heart-shaped herb bouquet is timeless, perfect for both bride and bridesmaid, as well as in miniature for a junior attendant or flower girl. It is also a lovely token for the young woman whose engagement is being announced. A bouquet of this style is held in the hand at the top or side. No handles are required.

A heart-shaped bouquet is easy to create, following this simple method of construction.

1. Wrap two 18-inch-long #20-gauge wires with white or colored florist's tape (A). (For a sturdier frame, use coat hanger wire or twist two pieces of wire together.)

2. Bend one wire to form slightly more than half a heart. (To determine the size you wish your finished heart to be, you may wish to cut out a paper heart and use that as the pattern over which to shape the wire.)

Steps in creating a heart-shaped wire base and covering it with short snippets of herbs and flower buds.

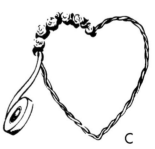

A   B   C

♥ Tie several herbal hearts together with a series of ribbons, and hang them on a mirror or front door.

♥ Use a miniature herbal heart, made with a lighter gauge wire, for a corsage or boutonniere.

♥ Use dried herbs and colorful flowers instead of fresh. Cover heart-shaped form with sheet moss, then use a glue gun to attach plant material.

3. Complete the heart shape by adding the second tape-covered wire. Join the two with a spiral twist (B). (Ready-made wire heart frames may be available at your local craft-supply shop.)

4. Select short snippets of herbs and flower buds, and fasten them to the frame with florist's tape. Sweetheart roses, wired hyacinth florets, stephanotis, and feathered carnations are some of the flowers that combine well with herbs. Tape each flower, or group of 2 or 3 flowers, on the front face of the heart in succession, working from the top center down one side, then the other. Always cover the stems of the flowers above with the heads of each succeeding herb and flower.

5. To give a graceful finish to the bouquet, add a velvet ribbon and herbal accent just off center near the base.

That love is all there is
Is all we know of love.
— Emily Dickinson

Herbal Hair Ornaments

With or without veiling, a crown of precious herbs and small flowers is an enchanting hair ornament. (See color photo, page 97.) As they have since ancient Roman times, brides (and bridesmaids) will be blessed with the wearing. Fragrant herbs and flowers on combs or barrettes or a wide-brimmed hat page 87) are extremely flattering to both little girls and big. Use a circlet of herbs to anchor veiling or attach the veiling to the back of the crown.

A thin wire coat hanger

White florist's tape

Conditioned herbs and
  flowers

3 yards narrow satin ribbon
  (or more)

White nylon tulle
  (optional)

Baby's-breath (optional)

Hair combs

Making a charmed circle is not difficult. A day or two before the wedding, gather your herbs and small flowers — rosebuds, clove pinks, lily-of-the-valley, violets, daisies, small zinnias, lilacs, mums, and many others. Condition them well in warm water for several hours (see pages 32–36). Be sure not to submerge the flowers. Several willing friends would be a great help if there are many halos to be made. Or, ask your florist to undertake this task as part of the wedding flowers project.

1. From the coat hanger, form a wire ring to fit the crown of the head. Cover it with white florist's tape. When working with florist's tape, stretch and pull it, smoothing it around the wire. This step could be done well in advance.

2. Cut all herb and flower stems to 2- to 3-inch pieces. Cut a few 3-inch pieces of ribbon and a few 4-inch squares of tulle.

3. Place an herb or two against the wire, and wrap it to the wire with florist's tape. Without cutting the tape, lay another snippet or two of herbs and flowers on the wire, overlapping the first one. Tape securely.

4. Continue on in this manner, always covering the stems of the herbs in place with the heads of those you are adding. Use a continuous piece of tape. Occasionally include a loop of ribbon and tuft of the net. Tuck in baby's-breath, too, if you wish. Work until the crown is well covered and balanced.

5. Complete the crown by attaching little bows of the ribbon here and there, or one bow with streamers at the back.

6. Attach hair combs in several places. Use combs with bendable attachments, or stitch them in place.

7. Spray very lightly with water. Keep the herbal halo in a plastic bag under refrigeration until needed. It will keep well for a day or two.

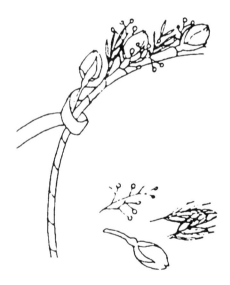

Wrap short-stemmed herbs and flowers to taped wire base, lapping each new piece over stems of preceding pieces.

MUSE'S ELYSIUM

A chaplet then of Herbs I'll make
Than which though yours be braver.
Yet this of mine I'll undertake
Shall not be short in savour.
With Basil then I will begin,
Whose scent is wondrous pleasing.
This Eglantine I'll next put in
The sense with sweetness seizing.
Then in my Lavender I lay
Muscado put among it,
With here and there a leaf of Bay,
Which still shall run along it.
Germander, Marjoram and Thyme,
Which uses are for strewing,
With Hyssop as an herb most prime
Here in my wreath bestowing.
Then Balm and Mint help to make up
My chaplet, and for trial
Costmary that so likes the Cup,
And next it Pennyroyal.
Then Burnet shall bear up with this,
Whose leaf I greatly fancy,
Some Camomile doth not amiss
With Savory and some Tansy.
Then here and there I'll put a sprig
Of Rosemary into it,
Thus not too Little nor too Big,
'Tis done if I can do it.

— Michael Drayton,
seventeenth-century
English poet

Combs with herbs and bows attached are another easy hair ornament, becoming to every member of the wedding. (See color photo, page 97.) Keep fresh herbs on combs enclosed in plastic under refrigeration until the last possible moment.

To construct, use the corsage and boutonniere technique described on the following pages to arrange small (or large) bunches of wedding flowers and herbs, fresh or dried, in your hand. Wire and tape them as instructed, then affix them to hair combs with florist's tape or ribbons and bows.

Easy Corsages and Boutonnieres

To make simple corsages and boutonnieres, flowers are wired to prevent their heads from falling off, to lighten the weight of the corsages, to retain existing moisture, and so that they can be maneuvered about on pliable new stems. Almost all wiring can be done with #24- or #26-gauge wire. Heavy stems or pine cones require heavier gauge wire, of course.

To wire many flowers, especially rosebuds, daisy types, and firm flowers, simply push the wire up through the calyx and center of the flower. If necessary, make a hook on the end of the wire, which you can then gently pull back down through the center until it is secured and no longer visible. Sometimes, such as with very heavy roses, daylilies, or gladiolus blossoms, it is best to use two crossed wires. Insert them through the bottom or calyx in a crossed fashion, then pull all the wires down to form a sturdy flexible stem. To give the ivy a longer, stronger stem, bend a piece of wire over into a hairpin-like hook, and pull it through the bottom of each leaf by poking both ends over the central vein. Pull the wire ends down along the natural stem and tape.

Cover all wires with florist's tape. Starting at the top of the wire stem, secure it firmly by turning the stem with one hand while gently pulling the florist's tape downward at a 30-degree angle. This releases the sticky substance that makes the tape adhere to itself. After a few practice sessions you will get the hang of it and be able to pull with one hand and twirl the stem with the other until all wire is concealed quickly and completely. In no time you will be taping a stem a minute.

Corsages

The following instructions are for a fairly elaborate corsage, suitable for mothers of the bride or groom. You may wish to make simpler versions for other honored guests. Following the instructions below, wire and tape one flower, from garden or florist, for each corsage. Cluster a few fragrant herbs around the flower, secure all stems with florist's tape, and tie on a small bow.

Keep all corsages refrigerated in a tightly covered container. Be sure to include corsage pins.

The mothers' corsages are sometimes better worn on a clutch bag or as a wristlet. If such is the case, fragrant herbs in

2 large, well-conditioned flowers, such as roses, carnations, chrysanthemums, gladiolus or yucca blossoms, asters, orchids, or gardenias

9 pieces of #26-gauge wire, in 8-inch lengths

2 large ivy leaves

Florist's tape

Assorted fragrant herbs, 3- to 5-inch sprigs

2 yards of #3 ribbon

2 corsage pins

Materials assembled for simple wired corsage.

or on the hands are heavenly to waft about on a hot summer's day.

Before you begin, be sure all cut flowers and herbs are well conditioned (see pages 32–36).

1. Tape all wires, reduce the stems of the large flowers to 1 inch, and wire them as described on page 52.

2. Wire the ivy leaves.

3. Place a wired and taped flower and ivy leaf **up.**

4. Place a wired and taped flower and ivy leaf **down.**

5. Tuck in several fragrant herb sprigs (no wire and tape necessary).

6. Tape them all together in the center. Twist the wire to secure, and cover it with a bit of tape again.

7. Tie a 12-inch piece of ribbon around the middle, over the wire and tape, knotting it in front.

8. Make a bow, and catch it in the piece of ribbon tied on in step 7.

9. Add two corsage pins. Spray. Wrap in plastic. Refrigerate until needed.

POCKET POSIES

Instead of conventional boutonnieres, consider "pocket posies," a handful of fragrant symbolic herbs gathered into a small bunch. If I am wearing a jacket with a breast pocket, I always stuff it with a casual bunch of herbs — mint, lavender, santolina, southernwood, scented geraniums, whatever. I pat it throughout the day, and it perfumes the air, alerts the senses as nothing else can, and constitutes aromatherapy. Dare to be different!

A generous handful of herbs for each groomsman, gathered in advance and kept fresh under refrigeration, is a wonderful added touch. Useful, too, when little things go wrong — and they always do. Just pat the fragrant pocket posies, breathe deeply, and relax.

Boutonnieres

A sprig of rosemary with a fluffy white carnation is always acceptable. You may instead wish to coordinate the boutonnieres with the bride's bouquet, and use a rose, daisy, or other flower. Another idea is to use a tiny bunch of herbs with a touch of lace and baby's-breath.

To make a simple boutonniere, follow instructions for the corsage (pages 53–54), but limit it to one ivy leaf, one flower of choice (to match the bridal party), and one sprig of herb, preferably rosemary (for remembrance) or myrtle (the emblem of love). Wire and tape all three components together, as described on pages 52–53. Keep them misted under refrigeration until needed. Baby's-breath or sweet Annie is optional, but don't forget a boutonniere pin!

Flowers for the Wedding Ceremony

Pew Bows

Use pew bows to mark seating for VIPs, or be more lavish and place an arrangement at every other pew for a truly dramatic setting.

In spring or summer, hang herb bunches upside down, as if to dry, so that if they wilt, they do so gracefully. In fall, when weather has conditioned them, arrange a casual handful of herbs upright in each bow.

Simple boutonniere

Foam-filled pew holders containing arrangements of fresh or dried herbs and flowers slip easily over the aisle-end of each pew.

A nifty gadget is designed especially for pew bows. It supports a round piece of floral foam that can be used wet with fresh herbs or dry for dried materials, so that the bows, herbs, and flowers can be quickly poked into place. The entire arrangement simply hangs over the edge of the pew by an attached hook, with absolutely no fiddling with wires, ribbons, or masking tape. The foam is replaceable, and the holders are reusable. Ask your local florist or craft shop if they are available, or see Mail-Order Sources on pages 181–182.

Large Bouquets for the Wedding Ceremony

Here is where a herb garden — yours or a friend's — comes into full play. We gather buckets of herbs, as long stemmed as possible, to condition in deep, warm water overnight out in the cool garage. As a rule of thumb, allow a bucketful per arrangement. (See also pages 33–36.) We set up a large, temporary table (plywood on sawhorses). We gather as many large vases as needed, fill them with well-dampened floral foam, put a pair of sharp pruners at the ready, and get to work a day or two before the wedding.

I like to use garden flowers or those purchased from a farmers' market. Order them in advance to be sure you will have enough and what you want. Count on a minimum of a dozen stems for each arrangement. Of course, your friendly florist will deliver flowers right to your door the day you need them. Or, take the herbs to the florist, if you are more comfortable having someone else do this project for you.

Herbs not abundant and long stemmed? Don't overlook tall roadside weeds, branches of leaves, or evergreens. There's a wealth of lovely plant material out there — daisies in late spring, tawny daylilies in summer, goldenrod in September. Harvest and enjoy.

Choose a dominance of white and light colors for their effect, but bear in mind that color harmonies can have the

Create oversize bouquets in large vases, beginning with a framework of your longest-stemmed material, then filling within that with herbs and foliage and finally the flowers. See directions on page 58.

most impact on your audience. With the wedding colors in mind, don't be afraid to add drama with a strong contrasting flower or perhaps bows.

Large arrangements start with suitable containers, perhaps vases borrowed from the church or synagogue. Vertical, horizontal, or triangular designs are traditional and easiest to accomplish, and they usually work well for these arrangements. Measure the space available, and plan accordingly, deciding in advance how many, how tall, and how wide the arrangements should be.

Basic flower arranging is a breeze if you follow these principles. They have worked successfully for years of teaching and practice. This is one of my favorite things to do.

1. Position the tallest and longest side stems first. Use a ruler if you need to. This is the skeleton; *never* extend outside this framework.

2. Fill in these outermost perimeters with slightly shorter materials, both herbs and foliage, fleshing out your pattern. Remember: Always stay within the original guidelines.

3. Tuck more herbs and greens in between. I call this the "poke-and-shove" method of flower arranging. Don't be afraid. Don't be timid. Although your bouquet may look sparse and funny at first, poke and shove to your heart's content. Be assured it will work. Continue to fill in the arrangement with full confidence that "and-just-one-more" is a proper attitude.

4. Fill in from behind as well as in front, angling materials as necessary to conform to your original basic pattern. Stems of varying length will give the proper fullness, depth, and dimension. The arrangement should **not** have the uniform appearance of a clipped hedge.

5. Finally, place your flowers strategically here and there, so that all their faces are visible and smiling at the couple taking their vows. If you have enough flowers, tuck a few in the back to complete your arrangement properly.

6. Add baby's-breath or bows last, if desired.

7. Mist thoroughly, swathe in sheets of plastic, and keep shaded and cool until your beautiful fragrant bouquets need to be transported to the location of the wedding.

If you are creating several arrangements for different locations around the church or synagogue, make them match, if at all possible. By following these same general instructions, and using a stepladder to reach your work, you can make 6-foot-tall arrangements, suitable for a cathedral or very large synagogue, if necessary, but I would advise practicing on smaller "buxom bouquets" first.

Herbs for the Reception

You'll want herbs and flowers in abundance at your reception, both for decorating the hall and tables and for garnishing the food itself. Be sure to make use of the flowers that were arranged for the ceremony. Unless wedding flowers are customarily left behind for other services, the ushers can recycle them on to the reception.

Instant Herbal Wreath around the Punch Bowl

Lay assorted sprigs of well-conditioned fresh herbs around the punch bowls. (It is considerate to serve both an alcoholic and a nonalcoholic punch, so be sure to gather enough herbs for two wreaths.)

To assemble your instant fresh herb wreath, cut 4- to 6-inch lengths of bright green curled parsley, grayed oregano, soft lamb's-ears, both green and gray santolina, pale marjoram, aromatic sweet Annie, all the basils, ferny southernwood, chartreuse lemon balm, mints of all kinds, rosemary in abundance, and/or scented geraniums. Clip a goodly assortment, and toss them in warm water in your sink to freshen them. Condition them well (see pages 32–36), drain them, and then pop the whole shebang into a large plastic bag, and keep it refrigerated until needed.

Scatter the herbs around the punch bowls at the last minute. If they are properly prepared, your fresh herbs will last through a long party without water. Top your punch with rings of ice containing lemon balm leaves, mint tips, roses, cherries, or strawberries (see page 159). Slices of lemon stuck with whole cloves are attractive spicy garnishes. Stir your punch with a very long cinnamon stick.

Herbs for the Wedding Cake

Ringed with snippets of fragrant herbs and colorful flowers, the cake will have the most beautiful setting possible. Prepare the herbs as just described for the punch bowl herbs. Put someone in charge of this special touch.

> As a symbolic gesture, strew rose petals and little snippets of herbs along the path of the bride. Just a few will do.

For the top of the cake, a charming nosegay is always pretty. Arrange the herbs in wet foam in a very small waterproof container painted white, and place it on top of the cake. Your florist will arrange this for you, too, if you provide the herbs you wish included.

For recipes and more information about wedding cakes, see chapter 8.

Strewing Herbs: A Centerpiece

In the temples in Biblical times and in dark monasteries and drafty castles during the Middle Ages, fragrant herbs were strewn on the floors to keep away creepie-crawlies, dispel the pestilence in the air, and make gatherings fragrant for people. So be it today — but with a difference.

Strewing herbs make easy-to-do centerpieces. Cut and condition (see pages 32–36) enough herbs for the number of tables at your reception. Keep them in a large plastic bag under refrigeration until needed. (It's good to have a spare refrigerator for this purpose.) Mobilize your committee of friendly neighbors and helpful family to "strew the herbs." Tell them

♥ where the herbs are kept under refrigeration;

♥ what time to "strew the herbs" — while the official photos are being taken and before the guests arrive;

♥ how to "strew the herbs" (anyone can do it, even children can help).

If your tables are round, use a circular motif. If they are long, strew the herbs in a serpentine line down the center. Lay down a "roadway" of lacy white paper doilies, flat leatherleaf fern from the florist (which is already conditioned), or flat lacy arborvitae pieces, 4 to 6 inches long, from the nearest hedge. (Condition arborvitae by tossing stems in a laundry tub of warm sugar water — 1 cupful of sugar to 1 gallon of water.) Allow them to remain overnight before draining the water, then store the greens in a plastic bag in a cool place for later use.

At the appointed time, lay the short snippets of fragrant herbs and colorful garden flowers or roses of your choice in place along the doily or leafy "roadway." Strew them along the front of the head table, as thickly or as thinly as your supply of herbs allows.

To ornament your centerpieces, include some little flowers, daisies, roses, or whatever is compatible with your wedding theme and color scheme. Here is where you tuck in paper fans, butterflies, "favorite things," white wedding balls, little baskets of mints, or just use bows assembled well in advance.

Add candlesticks, if you like, identical ones if you have enough, assorted-sized ones that are all silver or all glass, or low vigil lights in colorful glass containers — their glow resembles stained glass when lit.

Include small handwritten stand-up cards (see page 73) explaining the symbolism of the herbs in your "strewing herb centerpiece." Your guests will enjoy reading and knowing about the ancient plants you are using in your wedding theme.

Other Easy Centerpieces

Whether you use herbs and flowers en masse in huge full bunches or a single stem as a dramatic focal point, practice a bit, enjoy the challenge, and don't be intimidated by the floral part of the festivities. Here are some ideas.

Groupings of assorted-sized candles and candlesticks. Incorporate a few scented candles, too. Candles make a very simple and effective table decoration, bedded on cut herbs and greens, with a few flowers in florist picks of water for a finishing touch. Place each grouping on a base for easy placement and removal.

Mushroom baskets. These make practical centerpieces, and you should find them easily at your local supermarket. Midway around, tie each with pretty lace or ribbons, and fill the baskets with 3-inch pots of herbs, labeled. If you do this well in advance, line the basket with plastic and foil for carefree watering. Tuck in some excelsior or Spanish moss at the last minute. Add bows.

White milk-glass containers. Stark white is ideal for any wedding occasion, especially a bridal brunch. Collect white milk-glass bud vases of all sizes and shapes. I once found six in one hour spent at a local flea market. Fill the vases with single stems of herbs and assorted flowers, one of each to a vase. Arrange in groups down long tables or center several on round tables. This is charming and informal enough for any wedding herbfest.

Tussie-mussie centerpieces. Make a number of informal tussie-mussies, following the directions on pages 37–41. Attach them to tall supports (supported dowels or very tall wine bottles will work) with ribbons dangling midair. Groupings of these topiary-like bouquets are even more effective than single arrangements. Or, lay one atop napkin-covered boxes or flower pots that serve as pedestals to elevate them. **Note:** Let me give you a tip: Recycle any stray fragments of beauty or fragrance you can in these happy little bunches. It lends greater charm than you can imagine. And please don't lament what you see as a lack of professional craftsmanship! It's not at all essential — that is why they are so endearing.

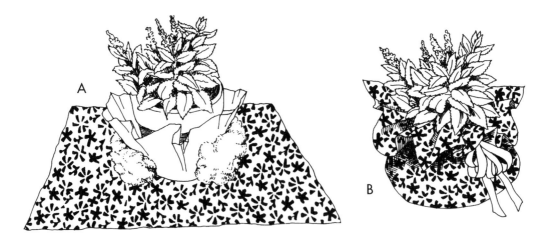

Create "soft sculpture" flower pots by (A) placing pot, foil, and batting on colorful fabric, then (B) bundling fabric around rim of pot and tying off with ribbon.

Elegant effects. Here is an idea suitable for after-four affairs. Collect assorted silver and glass antique bud vases and arrange them on mirrors, along with low vigil lights. Plain white warmer candles in clear glass tumblers add sparkle, too. Consider giving each lady guest a bud vase to take home as a token of your herbal wedding.

If time permits and you are so inclined, prepare bows with little white tags bearing the name and symbolism for each sprig of herb. They are guaranteed conversation at the party.

Table too narrow for centerpieces? Use wine glasses holding tiny herbal nosegays at each place.

Soft sculpture. Pots of herbs make entertaining center-pieces or favors. Cover the pots with plastic or foil, so they may be watered easily and kept alive. Then wrap each pot with batting or tissue to give it some puffiness, and set the pot on a square of calico fabric large enough to cover the pot. Gather the fabric up around the rim and tie it with contrast-ing ribbons or wool yarn.

Vegetable garden decor. Don't overlook the vegetable garden. Beautiful centerpieces can be created using vegetables,

MAKE-AHEAD BASES FOR CENTERPIECES

To make good use of time and scheduling, cut attrac-tive small-patterned evergreens, such as boxwood, juniper, Korean holly, and azalea, to use as bases for many last-minute fresh herb bouquets and decorations. Secure the heavy-stemmed evergreens in wet foam, covered and reinforced with chicken wire, if necessary. Keep the bases cool and misted for up to two weeks before the party or wedding. At the last minute, add well-conditioned sage, rosemary, lavender, rue, and southernwood, along with any colorful flowers you have. Bows (also finished weeks ahead) complete the arrangements.

A *floral foam-filled adapter allows you to wreathe each candlestick with fresh herbs and flowers.*

especially if you have a garden from which they may be gathered. Pick and polish whatever you have available. Have you ever studied a cabbage? It is a big, beautiful rose. Arrange a grouping of cabbages, partially opened, on a flat white wicker basket. Fill in with bunches of parsley, red basil, watercress, or your biggest heads of fragrant dill. Cover your table with a green-and-white patterned fabric, and use napkins of hot pink. Roll them into scrolls, tie with ribbon, and tuck in sprigs of rosemary. Stunning!

Eggplant can be dramatic, too, and peppers, red, green, and yellow, are jewels! If you don't grow your own, look over the display in your favorite market, then buy a great quantity of everything in season. Use them all through the house, as well as for an edible centerpiece fashioned in the Williamsburg manner.

Candlestick centerpieces. The prettiest herbal decoration is done with tall candlesticks and an adapter that holds damp floral foam and sits in any regular candle holder. (For sources, see page 182.) Charming arrangements of herbs are easily built in these candlestick containers. They can be done a day or two before the party and kept refrigerated.

To make a large number of centerpieces quickly, stuff the wet foam with 4-inch pieces of durable boxwood, ivy, or evergreens early in the week before the wedding. Keep them cool and damp. Closer to party time, tuck in well-conditioned herbs (see pages 32–36) and a few flowers. Bows in the wedding colors are pretty, too, and can be made well in advance. Fifty centerpieces — if you need that many — can be made fairly quickly by a few cooperative family members, including children. Be sure all the herbs, flowers, and evergreens are cut to the same length and that they are evenly distributed in the floral foam. We guarantee you the most attractive tables ever seen at a wedding — fragrant, too!

CHAPTER 4

Herbal Wedding Crafts

OR BRIDES — and friends and relatives of brides — who enjoy working with their hands, a wedding and all of the events associated with it provide dozens of opportunities to display their talents. In this chapter are some herb and needlecraft projects to get you started.

Wrap It Up

For bouquets, centerpieces, gift packages, decorations, tussie-mussies, and a hundred other little usages, bows are the crowning touch. Let me show you a foolproof way to make plump, perky bows. Begin by cutting 1 yard of any available satin ribbon. Now, follow the numbered steps on the next pages.

Madonna, wherefore hast
*   thou sent to me*
Sweet basil and mignonette?
Embleming love and health
*   which never yet*
In the same wreath might be.

— Percy Bysshe Shelley

MAKING A BOW

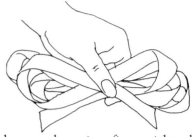

1. Near one end, make a 4-inch-long loop. Pinch it as tightly as possible between your left forefinger and thumb, as this is where you will tie the knot.

2. Make more loops in a figure eight, always pinching the "knot spot" in the center between the same two fingers. Go back and forth, up and down, as often as you like until you have as many loops as you want. Turn the ribbon as you work, so the right side (whether satin, velvet, or calico) is always on the outside.

3. If you want streamers, use additional yards of ribbon to make a few extra long loops to tuck in or to dangle freely. These loops can also be cut.

4. Secure the pinched central "knot spot" with wire, a pipe cleaner, or a narrow piece of ribbon. Trim the ends straight across in long, elegant points, or a bird tail V. For the bride's bouquet, "tie the knot" in the streamer ends.

Ribbon Roses

These pretty velvet ribbon roses are perfect with herbs. From boutonnieres to favors to herbal halos, they make easy, charming touches.

Make a right-angle fold in the center of a 30-inch piece of velvet ribbon (A). Fold the ends back and forth to the ends of the ribbon, as shown at B and C.

Hold ends and release folds. Now, as shown at D, grasp just one end (x) and release the other. Pull slowly on free end (y) until first or beginning fold almost disappears into center of flower (E). Tie ends together with thread or fine wire, which becomes your stem. Add a velvet rose leaf, if available, and tape the stem with florist's tape.

Ribbon rose

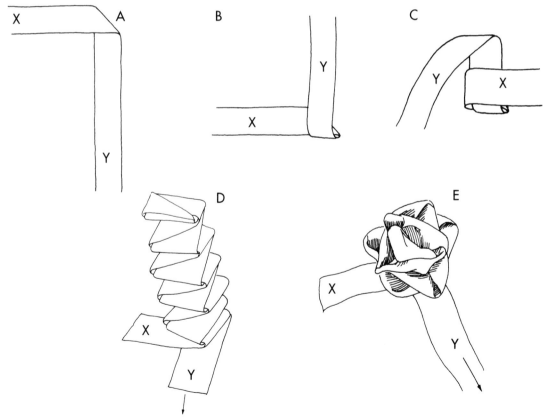

- Make bows into full pompoms by making eight or more loops on each side of the center pinched knot spot, all the same size.
- Graduate the bow loops from large to small for a formal effect.
- Make free-form loops of varied size for a more carefree bow.
- Bows are fun to do. Practice over and over until you get the idea!

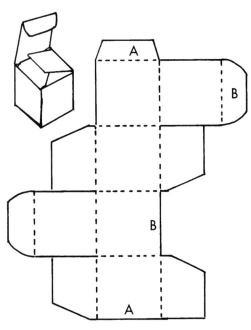

Pattern for box

Little Boxes

Little boxes can be useful for cake, rice, potpourri, bird seed, and favors of many sorts. Here's an easy-to-make old grade-school pattern to guide you. Use plain white sturdy paper that can be decorated or not, as you wish. Or, turn the project over to children who want to participate in the wedding preparations.

To make a box, enlarge the pattern and trace it onto stiff paper. Cut on straight lines and fold on dotted lines. Glue A to the inside of side A. Glue B to the inside of side B.

Herbal Wreaths

Herb wreaths are the loveliest of all decorations. If you want to set the scene with a joyous welcome, make wreaths up to a year in advance and use them many times over, throughout the prenuptial proceedings and for the wedding itself. Cut the herbs from your garden when it comes into its seasonal harvest. There is no more pleasant a task with greater rewards. Made well in advance, they can serve as fragrant decorations for your home, be laid flat on the reception tables, be hung on the doors of the house of worship — in fact, be used everywhere you want an attractive herbal touch. They make the best possible thank-you gifts for helpful family, friends, neighbors, and members of the wedding party. (See color photo, page 95.)

Even if you have only a mint patch, you can make a lovely fragrant wreath or two. An all-mint wreath is certainly possible and usually the most fragrant of all. Enjoy sniffing your hands after making your wreath! If your garden also contains lemon balm, sage, southernwood, tansy, or any of the silvery artemisias, you are in business. If you need additional material to eke out your supply, use cedar, boxwood, arborvitae tips, or evergreens from your foundation plantings. Avoid hemlock, yew, and spruce, greens that drop their needles. Cut a large basket full of snippets. The cuttings need be only 6 inches long. You'll fill your house with fragrance while you work on this project.

Supplies are truly minimal. You will need a box-type four-ring wreath frame, 10 or 12 inches or larger, and a spool of sturdy carpet thread in any neutral color.

Begin by wrapping the wreath ring with leftover scraps of ribbon (recycled big bows from gift boxes will do nicely) or strips of leftover fabric cut on the bias with pinking shears.

Secure the beginning and end of the wrappings with straight pins or staples. Covering the wreath's frame first prevents light from passing through the completed dried wreath. Herbs are fleshy when fresh, never heavy as pinecones or

VICTORIAN FANTASY BOUQUET

Combine Ribbon Roses (page 67), laces, ribbons, dried flowers, and herbs in a cluster. Add anything — birds and butterflies, buttons and bows. Wrap the bundle in vintage crocheted doilies or velvet. Pin this romantic bouquet on broad-brimmed hats, fans, muffs, baskets, or all-green herbal wreaths. These irresistible wedding accessories are endlessly useful. A drop of essential oil here and there brings the cluster to life.

evergreens. As they dehydrate, they lose their density. Wrapping the wire wreath ring is important, but what you use is immaterial, since it doesn't show.

Start anywhere and lay a small handful of assorted herbs (six to ten stems) against the ring. Attach a length of thread to the frame. (Do not cut thread from spool.) With the spool held firmly in your hand, secure the herbs in place by bringing the thread through the center of the wreath form several times.

Place a second, similar bunch so that it covers the stems of the preceding bunch. Wrap them in place by pulling the thread tightly around them, as before. Continue on around the ring in this manner until it is totally covered. Lay the bunches on quite thickly, covering the base as much as possible. The bow will be placed where the first and last bunches of herbs join, so don't worry if it seems a little flat there.

The bunches can be as varied as you like. Use everything your garden yields. The loveliest wreath of all is en-

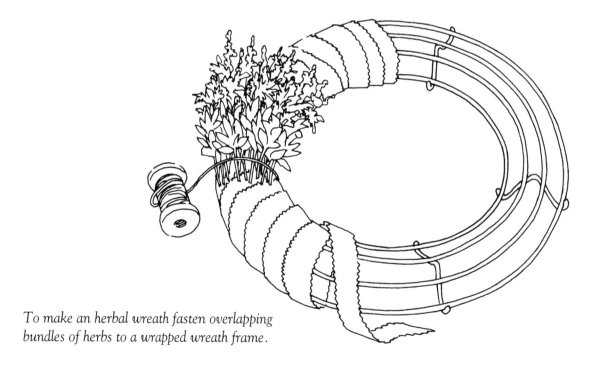

To make an herbal wreath fasten overlapping bundles of herbs to a wrapped wreath frame.

tirely silver herbs, if you have enough silver plants to do this. Ornamented with silvery lunaria, pearly everlasting, white feverfew flowers, baby's-breath, and white velvet bows, a silver wreath makes an elegant wedding decoration.

The next day, when your herbs begin to dry and shrivel, snip off drooping tips or any heavy stems that protrude. Tuck in additional material, if necessary — it's easy to do.

Allow the wreath to dry several days lying flat in a warm, dry place, preferably out of strong light. The fragrance of the drying wreath is heavenly, so place it where you can enjoy it during the process. Once it is dry, hang it on the kitchen wall and enjoy it.

Now your imagination can take over. If your herb garden has produced seed heads, such as bee balm, hyssop, tansy buttons, or golden yarrow, mint spikes, lavender flowers, the knotted marjorams, dill heads, or any dried flowers, gather all you can and poke them down into the wreath. No need to wire the herbs and flowers on picks. They have sturdy stems that will be caught in the network of dried herbs and threads. You can't believe how easy this is until you have done it. If you want to include fragrant spices in your wreath, you will need to wire and tape these onto floral picks to insert them into the herbs, or sometimes they can be glued in place.

No herb garden? Herbs of the fields and roadsides are free for the gathering. Goldenrod, Joe-Pye weed, boneset, pearly everlasting, staghorn sumac, catnip, dock, Queen-Anne's-lace, and many other wild herbs of the field are welcome additions. Tuck in strawflowers, 'Fairy' roses if they are available (use these fresh and let them dry on the wreath), eucalyptus, and any other dried materials you might like to add. Make your wreath as pretty and colorful as possible.

Your wedding wreaths can all be alike or each different, depending upon where you plan to use them and the materials you have available. It is best to group similar wreaths in the same general area. Harmonize them by attaching "favorite things," if you've a chosen theme, or by using a single color or identical bows.

WEDDING FLOWER WREATH

The most sentimental of all wreaths is the one created from the wedding flowers. Dry them (or ask someone to dry them for you while you are on your honeymoon), and then attach them to a wreath frame. These will make a wonderful decoration for your new home and a keepsake to love and cherish forever.

A bow (see page 66) will complement and complete your herbal wreath. Make it full and perky, in white for the wedding, and then change it later to coordinate with a room or a season.

You will enjoy your beautiful fragrant herb wreaths for a long time after the wedding is over. They can be added to, refreshed, and used for years.

For more information about wreathmaking, see my *Wreaths...of all Sorts* in Mail-Order Sources (pages 181–182).

Quickie Spice Wreaths

These adorable aromatic wreaths can be created in miniature to use as favors or made large to serve as decorations. Purchase small (3- or 4-inch) Styrofoam rings at any craft shop (or cut them out of cardboard), and wrap them with brown florist's tape or textured fabric. Attach a small hanger at the back.

Cover your wreath generously with Tacky Glue. Embed bay leaves; small nuts, pinecones, or acorns; bits of cinnamon

For an aromatic miniature wreath, attach a variety of dried pods and spices to a small wreath form.

bark; vanilla beans; whole aniseed, dill, cumin, caraway, poppyseeds — anything dried from your herb garden or spice cupboard. Whole cloves and star anise are both fragrant and attractive. For color, glue on cardamom, dried orange peel, petals, rose hips, candied ginger, pistachios, whatever is available. Look around you, especially on the spice shelf in your favorite store, with an eye toward color, size, shape, and texture as well as fragrance.

Once all these ingredients are assembled, you can make many spicy wreaths. Why not organize a workshop?

Fasten on a bow, if you wish. Allow your wreath to dry thoroughly before hanging.

Styrofoam balls can be covered the same way and used as topiary decorations.

Invitations and Place Cards

Invitations. No herbal invitations available at your stationery store? No pressed herbs to create your own? No time for such handwork? Use a piece of tracing paper to draw the handmade invitation shown on page 74, filling in appropriate names, date, and place. It can be enlarged to 8½" x 11", folded, and mailed without an additional envelope.

Helen's pop-ups. This simple pop-up place card can carry a name, a good-luck wish, or a herb and a note about herbal

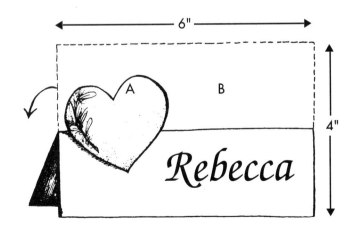

Cut out top of heart from A to B, so that it stands up when card is folded. Glue a small sprig of herbs at the top.

symbolism. It can also be an invitation or clever thank-you card. Use pumpkins for fall, trees for Christmas, eggs for Easter, or hearts any time. The card is best devised from sturdy white paper, such as watercolor paper. Color the pop-up a contrasting color. Once folded, it stands smartly at attention.

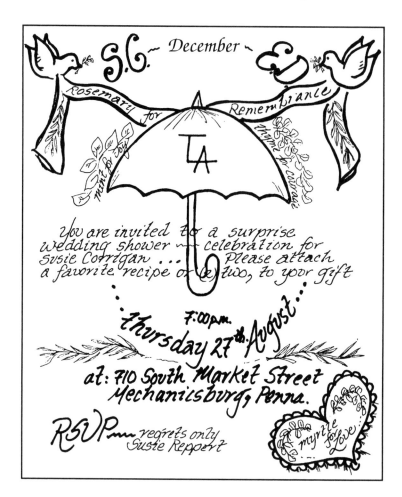

Sample shower invitation.

"A Joy Forever" — Ways to Preserve Your Wedding Bouquet

A lovely bride and beautiful flowers are the combination that makes a wedding a thing of beauty. Photographs and gowns packed away in lavender are tangible mementos. But what of the fragile wedding flowers? Like all living things, they are, alas, perishable. But don't let that deter you. Keep your beautiful flowers for as long as you like — dried, pressed, or in fragrant potpourri — a timeless keepsake to cherish and an heirloom for the future.

It's very satisfying to preserve the wedding flowers. Furthermore, you have a choice of ways to do it, none of them difficult. Use any or all of the methods suggested, depending upon the amount of flowers available.

Drying the Wedding Bouquet

Arrange with your florist to have a small bouquet to toss, so you can preserve your wedding herbs and flowers to decorate your first home. Request flowers that are foolproof for drying, such as chrysanthemums, carnations, and roses. Gladiolus and orchids are extremely difficult to preserve, although possible as long as you don't expect them to look as dewey-fresh as the original.

Since best results are achieved by working with the flowers and herbs as soon after the ceremony as possible, perhaps one of your attendants or a clever craft-minded relative will take care of this for you, if the necessary equipment has been assembled before hand.

To dry flowers, there are several important things to remember. First, keep them dry; second, get to the project as quickly as possible, before the flowers fade. If it cannot be

Wedding portrait of Ottylie Elgert and Gustav Peplau, who were wed on February 12, 1907 (drawn by their granddaughter Marjorie Louise Reppert).

Lay flower heads on a base of silica gel, and pour more silica gel gently over to cover them.

done immediately, keep the flowers cool and dry, wrapped in plastic, in a refrigerator. With luck, they will keep well for up to a week.

To preserve your wedding flowers in three-dimensional loveliness, you will need a box of silica gel (a commercial product available under several trade names) and a tightly covered container. Take apart the bride's bouquet and reduce the stems to 2 inches. Boutonnieres, reception flowers, attendants' bouquets, decorations from the wedding service, and cake tops can be done the same way. Bury each flower in the silica gel, following instructions that come with the product. Seal the lid from air with masking tape. In less than a week your flowers will be dry and permanently preserved. Spray them with clear plastic or shellac to prevent shattering and the disastrous effects of humidity.

Another way to dry the flowers is to use sterilized playbox sand, available from hardware stores or building suppliers. Be sure it's playbox sand and not builders' sand, which has sharp edges that will cut the petals. Pour a layer of sand in a shoe box, carefully embed the flower heads or herbs of your choice in the sand, and cover completely with another layer of sand. The flowers should not touch each other. After a week in a warm, dry place, most flowers will be dry enough for fragile permanence behind glass.

After the flowers are dry by either method, they can be reassembled as they were, arranged in a container to ornament your new home, incorporated into a herbal wreath (see pages 69–73), or — my preference — glued in a deep frame under glass along with the newspaper announcement of the engagement, the wedding announcement, or the wedding invitation and the bride's portrait. No matter the degree of artistry, this thoughtful gift will be a favorite.

A Pressed Flower Arrangement

If you prefer pressing your flowers to drying them whole, you can combine them with the wedding invitation to frame and hang in a prominent spot in your new home. This project also makes a treasured gift. Any frame will work well. Select a background (perhaps a scrap of the wedding dress), mount the wedding invitation on it, and arrange a floral wreath of the pressed dried flowers and herbs around it in an attractive design. After you have the composition to your satisfaction, use white glue or any clear-drying adhesive to keep it in place, and replace the glass. (See color photo, page 93.)

A Bridal Potpourri of Scent and Sentiment

If you would rather not whisk your wedding flowers out of sight to be dried because you want to enjoy them fresh for as long as possible, you can always convert them into potpourri. Any of the wedding flowers that aren't pressed or haven't dried successfully — flowers from the wedding party, the reception, the bridal bouquet, the boutonnieres, corsages worn by mothers — can be air-dried and turned into the fragrant mixture called *potpourri*.

HOW TO PRESS HERBS AND FLOWERS

The secret to the successful pressing of flowers is to provide even distribution of weight on the books containing the flowers and — most important — frequently changing the absorbent papers between flowers. I use white facial tissues or blotting paper, which rapidly absorbs moisture from the flowers. If the tissues are not changed, the moisture flows back into the drying flowers, turning them very dark. For best color, change the absorbent papers every three days. A flower press is nice, but old telephone books are all you need, if they are well weighted.

Certain "fat" flowers, such as roses, do not flatten very easily; remove outside petals, and press them separately. Daisies, bouvardia, stephanotis, violets, and other thin-petaled flowers are better subjects for pressing. Be sure to press some of the foliage, especially ferns.

Whenever I do the flowers for a wedding, I save and air-dry left-over flowers to make an ultra-special potpourri for the newlyweds' new home. Sometimes I dry a few of the bride's flowers in silica gel (see page 76) or press some petals and herbs (see page 77). I then frame these sentimental mementos with the wedding invitation or announcement and present them to the couple long after the wedding is over.

The ancient art of making potpourri lends itself to the preservation of traditional wedding flowers. It is a rich combination of scent and sentiment.

You can add other treasured flowers to your collection — prom corsages, engagement roses, shower centerpieces, Valentines. And, you can add to your mixture in the future with anniversary bouquets and, eventually, Mother's Day tributes — that's looking ahead!

After you have gleaned all the enjoyment from them, pull the faded flowers apart. Don't overlook the foliage as you work. If the flowers are not absolutely dry, spread them out on a clean sheet of paper and let the air complete the work for you. They **must** be absolutely dry — "chip" dry.

When the petals feel crunchy to the touch, go to your nearest herb shop to obtain a little bottle of essential oil and some orrisroot, a modest investment.

The orrisroot will act as a fixative for the fragrances, and the oil of your choice will make your wedding flowers smell heavenly. Add approximately ¼ cup orrisroot to 1 quart of petals and 6 to 12 drops (or more) of oil, and stir. Place in a covered container to blend and mellow. Stir occasionally over a period of a month or so, adding dried orange peel, spices, your wedding herbs, or more oil, if you want to increase the fragrance.

Placed in an attractive covered jar, your wedding flowers will perfume your room and your life whenever you wish. Open the jar full of fragrant wedding flowers to release its perfume; close it when not in use to renew and preserve the fragrance for all the years of your marriage.

A Bride's Basic Potpourri

Combine all ingredients and place in a tightly covered plastic container for several weeks. Stir occasionally, and add more oil if you wish the scent to be stronger. Put the finished product in a pretty jar to enjoy for many years.

1 quart rose petals or scented herbs, dried thoroughly

3 tablespoons ground orrisroot

8 drops rose oil

A Forty-Year-Old Rose Jar Recipe

Dry the rose petals, and mix them with the salt. Stir the spices, lavender flowers, toilet water, oil, and orrisroot into the dried rose petals. Age in a tightly covered tin for several weeks before putting the mixture in a decorative container to perfume your new home.

Rose petals (or wedding flowers), dried

¼ cup Kosher salt

¼ ounce each ground cloves, mace, and allspice

½ ounce ground cinnamon

¼ pound lavender flowers

¼ ounce toilet water or cologne (preferably lavender)

A few drops of rose oil

2 ounces ground orrisroot

My Favorite Potpourri

Mix everything together. (The oil and orrisroot can be mixed together and added last.) Stir. Store in a closed jar for 2 to 4 weeks until well blended. Put in a pretty jar for your living room. Open and stir when you want to enjoy the fragrance of your wedding herbs and flowers.

1 quart dried wedding herbs and flowers

½ cup patchouli

¼ cup sandalwood chips

¼ cup vetiver roots

1 teaspoon each frankincense, myrrh, ground cloves, ground cinnamon

1 tonka bean, finely chopped

¼ cup ground allspice

10 drops rose oil

1 cup ground orrisroot

Sachets

When you use the French word *sachet* you mean *in a little bag*. The only difference between potpourri and sachet is just that. You have put some potpourri "in a little bag" or small sack.

Sachet favors. Use a 6-inch square of organdy, satin, calico, or tulle in your choice of color. Pile potpourri in the center, draw up the sides to surround a ball of potpourri, and secure with a 12-inch piece of narrow ribbon. Tie a bow. Catch a little flower or sprig of rosemary in the bow. Arrange the corner points of the square into lively puffs. Made long in advance of the festivities, these can be stored in covered boxes lined with white wrapping tissue to preserve their fragrance until party time.

Paper sachets. These are perfect for your paper (first) anniversary. Fold colorful papers into packets, and fill with strongly scented potpourri. Glue the sachets to paper lace doilies, round or square or both together. Add tiny ribbons, floral seals, and a dash of glitter. Reminiscent of old-fashioned valentines, these are fun to make. If you wish you can use them for invitations or favors.

Keepsake sachets. Make them of lace, tulle, calico, or the fabric used to make the bridesmaids' dresses. Select herbs you plan to use in the wedding — roses, lavender, mint, sage, rosemary, and so on. Combine the dried herbs together with oil and fixatives to make a fragrant potpourri mixture (see page 79) to give as sachet favors at the rehearsal dinner for the close family and wedding party. Whether you stitch up little pillows or make your sachets out of 6-inch squares of material, tie them with a bow (see pages 65–66).

Sachet centerpiece. Select a graceful branch or branches, and secure in a flowerpot (or any container) with plaster of paris. A few rocks in the bottom will give the pot weight and stabilize your centerpiece. Stitch heart sachets (see pages 83–84) of calico or lace, fill them with fragrant potpourri, and hang the sachets on the branches. They will grace your table and make delightful favors, too. Not good at stitchery? Buy metal tea balls — the kind you use to make a pot of tea — fill with potpourri and tie them onto the branches with little bows.

Ice-cream cone sachets. Buy real cones or devise cornucopias from circular pieces of stiff paper. Make sachet balls by filling 6-inch squares of pastel fabric with ⅓ cup potpourri. Tie each square firmly into a plump, rounded ball and place it, rounded side up, into the cone. Fruit-flavored oils are always a winner.

Lollipop sachets. Small sachet balls can be tied with bows to lollypop sticks as novel favors. These are cute decorations tied to a Christmas tree.

Sachet nosegays. These sachets use pipe cleaners for "stems." One large sachet ball centered in a round, lacy paper doily is a charming small souvenir. Or, make several smaller sachet balls and cluster them together. Complete the nosegays by adding bows with streamers.

Ice-cream cone sachet

Lollipop sachet

Lavender — "to lay away the wedding gown." Store your treasured garment properly for your children and your children's children. Professionals advise a dark, dry, cool or airy place. Have the dress cleaned so all dust is removed before it is laid away in acid-proof blue tissue paper — lots and lots of it — then sealed in a covered box. Before you seal it, however, place flat sachet pillows filled with a pound of lavender blossoms (grown in your garden or purchased) nestled in the tissue paper to protect your cherished memento from moths and to keep it as fresh and fragrant as the day you said "I do."

2 pieces of calico fabric, 10" x 10"

One 8-inch and one 22-inch length of ½-inch lace and coordinating thread

One 12-inch pipe cleaner

¼ cup fragrant potpourri

One narrow satin ribbon (12 inches long)

1. Enlarge the pattern below, and use it to cut two calico pieces.

2. With wrong sides of calico together, stitch sides, taking ¼-inch seams. Turn right side out, and press.

3. Hand or machine stitch the 22-inch length of lace around the top edge, lace ruffles upward. Hand stitch the 8-inch length of lace around the bottom edge, lace ruffles downward. Be careful not to stitch across the bottom opening.

4. Insert the pipe cleaner down the middle of the parasol, so that approximately 2 to 3 inches show at the bottom. Stitch in place across the bottom.

5. Gather the bottom with basting stitches and pull closed. Secure with tiny stitches.

6. Stuff the parasol with your favorite potpourri.

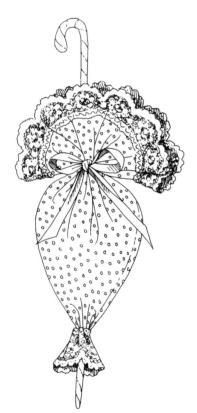

Potpourri-filled parasols make desirable party favors.

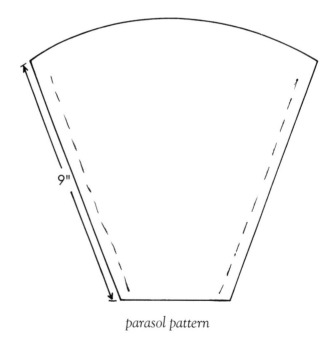

9"

parasol pattern

7. Baste around the top, gather to close, and hand stitch, securing with tiny stitches. Tie the narrow satin ribbon in place just below the lace edge, and make a bow.

8. Bend the upper portion of the pipe cleaner to form the handle.

Vicki's Heart Sachets

A dear, clever friend has given us an original, easy-to-stitch heart sachet, a simple little pattern that's worth its weight in gold. Make these potpourri bags as gifts from the bride to her attendants. They can be filled with flowers in the colors that match the attendants' dresses, such as pink rosebuds, purple lavender, pale green lemon verbena, blue bachelor's-buttons, or yellow jasmine. Tie the bottoms with ribbon to match and — voilà! — you have a pretty heart sachet, the most useful wedding party accessory you can make.

Two 6" x 16" pieces of tulle

18 inches of ½-inch lace

4 inches of ⅛-inch ribbon (for loop)

12 inches of ⅛-inch ribbon (for bow/tie)

6-strand embroidery thread

1. Enlarge the drawing below to use as a pattern.

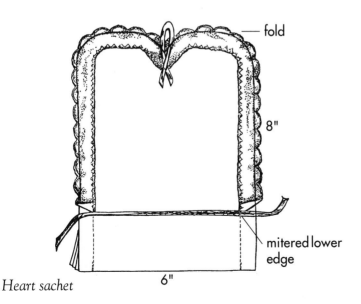

fold

8"

mitered lower edge

Heart sachet   6"

Any of these sachets can be made with cotton balls and essential oils as well as with potpourri. Remember, however, that the balls must be 100 percent cotton. Synthetics repel the oils, and your dear little favors will lose their scent quickly if you use anything other than cotton balls.

2. Lay one piece of tulle against the other, and fold them to form a 6" × 8" rectangle.

3. Taking a ½-inch seam, sew along one long side, across the top, following the pattern, and down the other side. Use a straight stitch. Include the 4-inch piece of ribbon in a loop at the center top. Leave the bottom open.

4. Using a slight zigzag stitch, sew lace over the ½-inch seam allowance to cover it. Sew to within 2 inches of the bottom edge. Miter the lower edge of the lace, as shown.

5. Stuff with potpourri.

6. Loosely baste the bottom edge using six-strand embroidery thread. Pull to gather and close. Conceal the gathering stitches with the 12-inch piece of ribbon tied in a bow.

Bride's Heels

Four 4" × 2" pieces of white satin

Embroidery thread or fabric paint

2 sachets

Here's a vintage touch for a wedding, pure Victoriana — a pair of white satin, cotton-stuffed heel pads for the bride's slippers, to be worn on her wedding day.

Making bride's heels may take all day, but they will be a highly personal gift or keepsake. "Here comes the bride . . . tum tum ta tum . . . ."

left heel   right heel

Use these drawings as patterns for Bride's Heels.

1. Enlarge the pattern to fit the heel of the bride's shoe (pattern is about half size).

2. Use the adjusted pattern to cut four pieces out of the satin. Be sure to allow for seams.

3. Embroider or paint the lily-of-the-valley design around the edge and the four-leafed clover, as shown.

4. Put the bride's initials and the month and day of the wedding on the left heel and the groom's initials and the year on the right heel.

5. Tuck sachet between the pieces of satin for each heel, then blanket stitch around the edge. (I like to use moss green embroidery thread for this.)

LAWN HERBS FOR LUCK

Clover not only symbolizes protection to the household, but also a prosperous, joyous, long marriage with great happiness and good fortune. No bride should go down the aisle without three-leafed clovers for love or four-leafed clovers for luck in both shoes!

Fan-Shaped Ring Pillow

This different little ring pillow is simple to make. Made in material that matches the bride's gown, it is a lovely handmade keepsake.

1. Enlarge the drawing on page 86 to use as a pattern.

2. Cut two pieces of fabric following the pattern.

3. Put the two pieces together, right sides facing. Sew the two straight side seams, taking a ¼-inch seam allowance. Turn right side out.

Satin or moire fabric (two pieces, 6" x 8½")

2 yards white satin ribbon

18 inches ruffled white lace

7 white silk or dried flowers (or ribbon roses — see page 67)

Cotton stuffing (or potpourri)

4. Sew on the pattern dotted lines to create the divisions of the fan.

5. Stuff each section lightly with cotton or potpourri.

6. Turn the scalloped edges in, and hand sew with tiny stitches.

7. Stitch ruffled lace along scalloped edge. Tack a white flower at the top of each segment. Tack a small piece of ribbon to the center of the pillow, so that rings may be loosely tied on. Attach ribbon to the bottom of fan for hanging streamers. Dab a bit of perfume oil on the back of the padded fan.

A fan-shaped ring pillow is a lovely keepsake.

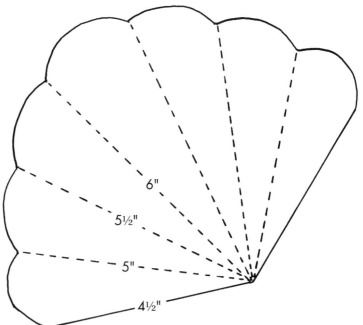

6"

5½"

5"

4½"

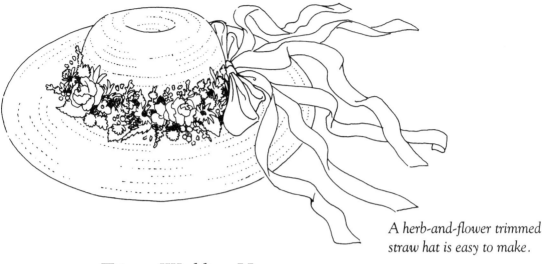

A herb-and-flower trimmed straw hat is easy to make.

Trim a Wedding Hat

Straw hats trimmed with herbs and dried flowers are perfect accents for summer garden weddings. They are stunning, yet easy to do. Each hat will take about an hour of time.

1. Glue the yard of ribbon around the crown of the hat, allowing for long streamers in back. Tie on the streamers using the narrow piece of ribbon. Because of the contour of the crown, the ribbon will not be smooth. No matter, it will be well covered in the next steps.

2. Dab glue on top of the hat band, and pat moss in place. The moss gives you a textured bed in which to nestle your flower heads and herbs.

3. Put glue in a small dish, and, one by one, dab each flower and herb in glue, then fix into place around the crown. You can start with large flowers and taper out on both sides toward the back, or place small matching clusters at several equidistant points, or simply glue the floral material on hit-or-miss. Of course, you can do this with a glue gun.

4. Attach a pretty bow in back.

Straw hat of your choice

1 yard #9 satin ribbon

½ yard #3 satin ribbon

Small piece Spanish moss

Colorful dried flowers and herbs, your choice (consider dried fruit slices, pomegranates, pepperberries, etc.)

More ribbon for bow and streamers

About 3 yards #9 satin ribbon

Tacky Glue

Herbal Wedding Rice

Dear, dear doctor,
What will cure love?
Nothing but the clergy,
And white kid glove.

— *Folklore of Love and*
Courtship

It once was believed that evil spirits always appeared at weddings and that by throwing rice at the married couple the spirits were appeased and they would do no harm to the newlyweds.

The custom of throwing rice is celebrated the world over. Rice in some form has always played an important part in wedding ceremonies. Sometimes the bridal couple eat it together as a symbol of their living together; sometimes it is sprinkled over them, symbolizing fruitfulness. Hindus throw rice that is perfumed with patchouli and other native exotic scents.

Instead of exotic perfumes, I suggest adding dried rosemary and, especially in June, dried rose petals — roses to symbolize love and rosemary for remembrance.

Use rosemary from your pantry shelf if you do not have a plant to harvest. Dry the rose petals, either by air-drying on a screen or in an oven at 150°F for 30 minutes. Pink and red roses dry the most effectively. Add the chip-dry rose petals and rosemary to the rice in generous quantities. You can even cook and serve this wedding rice, as all the ingredients are edible.

Place a large bowl of the wedding rice mixture where the guests can help themselves to a handful, or present it in a basket in pretty individual packets of net or organdy tied with ribbons that harmonize with the wedding colors. Ask two young friends or relatives to distribute the rice packages after the ceremony. Tie a bunch of herbs on the handle of the basket. We like to attach little cards to the individual rice packets. Your guests will be enchanted by the colorful and fragrant addition of rosemary and rose petals. The ancient symbolism will anoint the newlyweds with all kinds of beautiful good wishes.

You may color wedding rice with vegetable-dye food coloring, if you wish. Make a glassful of a deep-colored dye solution and pour it over the white rice. Strain and reuse the dye bath until you have made as much colored rice as desired. It's amazing how quickly the dry rice absorbs color. Dry the rice thoroughly on thick newspapers before adding herbs or packaging. The Rosemary House offers "Mail-a-Herb" cards in which to package wedding rice (see Mail-Order Sources, page 182). **Caution:** The dyed rice is not colorfast and may run in rainy weather.

> If there are objections to throwing rice, simply substitute birdseed. Our feathered friends will clean it up while they feast.

Nancy Reppert's Wedding Rice Roses

Make a basketful of roses to hold the wedding rice. Poke the roses into a basket with Styrofoam on the bottom to help stabilize the roses and prevent the contents from spilling. If you make these well in advance of the wedding, tuck a small piece of paper towel in the top of the roses after filling them to prevent spilling. Remember to remove the papers prior to presenting the roses to the wedding guests.

1. As shown at A, prepare the wire stem for each rose by forming a ¼-inch loop at one end of the wire. Beginning just below the loop, completely cover the stem with florist's tape, pulling and stretching the tape as you go to release the adhesive from the tape. Halfway down, wrap the leaf in with the tape to attach it to the stem. For variety, add other leaves along the stem, if you wish.

Organdy, satin, calico, or other fabric, 4½" x 4½"

Coordinating thread

8-inch piece of #26 heavyweight wire

Green florist's tape

Green cloth leaf, 1½ to 2½ inches long (or ribbon folded to resemble a leaf)

♥ A basket of these roses makes an easy dual-purpose centerpiece for any bridal party, including the reception.

♥ Make half "his" color and half "her" color, and pass them out to "his" and "her" family and friends before the wedding.

♥ An informal committee can make dozens of wedding rice roses well in advance — another fun party.

2. To prepare the rose, fold the fabric square in half, right sides together (B). Using a ¼-inch seam, stitch the length of the 4½" side to form a tube. Turn the material right side out. Press. (For a rose factory operation, sew 'em all in one row — backstitch, then snip apart!)

3. To attach the tube to the prepared stem (C), insert the looped end of the wire into the base of the tube. Not too far! Pinch the base tightly, and use very short stitches to secure the material to the wire. With florist's tape, cover the gathered material and stitches and secure them to the stem.

4. At the top of the rose, fold a 1-inch hem inward to form a pocket. Fill the pocket with wedding rice with rosebuds and rosemary (see pages 88–89) or birdseed.

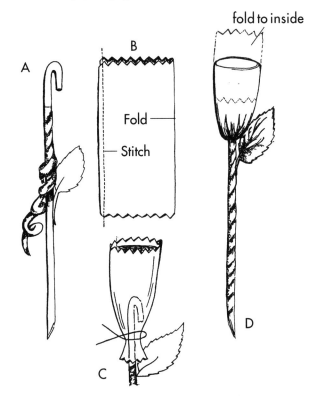

Crisp Caraway Cookies
(page 140) with engage-
ment announcement

Tussie-mussie favors (page 41)

An example of "favorite
things" used as decorative
focal points

Framed wedding invitation (pages 77-78)

NICHOLAS WHITMAN

(from the left) Herbwiches (page 168),
Lemon Balm Jelly (page 154) with crackers,
Tomato-Rose Hip Aspic (page 123)

(clockwise from top) Fruit Strata (page 127), Italian Love Cake (page 134), Violet Pinwheels (page 177), and Rose-Petal Sandwiches (page 177); (inset) Lavender Favor (page 107)

94 ♥

A fresh herbal wreath (pages 69-72)

A bride's Clutch Bouquet (page 44)

Basket of rose petals

(left) Hair Comb with dried herbs and flowers (page 52)
(right) Herbal Halo (pages 49-50)

*Wedding cake trimmed
with roses and
lavender*

CARRIE GREENE

Cake server trimmed with herbs

*Guest book and herb
bouquet*

CHAPTER 5

Wedding Customs

LIKE OTHERS of life's most beloved celebrations, weddings are surrounded by myriad traditions and symbols. Herbs may be used with many of these ancient lucky charms, amulets, and symbolic customs to make your wedding that much more memorable. In this chapter you will read about some of the very familiar as well as some little-known customs from all over the world, throughout history. You will also read about some very special weddings that I have been privileged to be part of.

Something old. "Something old, something new; something borrowed, something blue." In England, they add, "And a sixpence in her shoe." (Need a six pence? — see Mail-Order Sources, pages 181–182.) Wearing some piece of clothing from an older woman who is happily married is meant to transfer that good fortune to the new bride. It is a form of "sympathetic magic." Traditionally, the something borrowed should be golden because gold indicates the sun, the source of life.

*All dear Nature's
children sweet
Lie 'fore bride and
bridegroom's feet,
Blessing their sense!...*

— John Fletcher,
"Bridal Song"

♥ Ancient Roman
brides carried
bunches of herbs
under their wedding
veils.
♥ The Saracens carried
orange blossoms as a
symbol of fertility.
♥ An Austrian custom
is to cross the veil
with a wreath
of fresh myrtle,
ancient flower of
love.

Orange blossoms. These traditional wedding flowers come from an evergreen tree and are therefore believed to stand for everlasting love. Because the tree blossoms and fruits at the same time, it is considered particularly lucky.

Wheat wreath. In Europe, brides once wore wreaths of grains or wheat. Both of these emblems of fertility, to insure large families.

Chuppah. Since the sixteenth century, Jewish couples have been married under the traditional Chuppah — a wedding canopy of cloth suspended from four posts. The Chuppah can be quite simple or lavishly decorated with flowers and greenery. It is sometimes carried from the sanctuary to become a focal point for the head table at the wedding reception.

Wedding veils. A custom taken from the Near East, wedding veils are part of the custom of purdah, which requires that women wear a covering to conceal all but their eyes. It is also supposed to be symbolic of the canopy once held over the bridal couple to protect them from the "evil eye."

Lover's knot. This knot has been a marriage emblem from remotest times. The bride's bouquet is usually decorated with ribbons in which the knots are tied. Because wishes are supposed to be held by a knot, many knots are needed to hold all the good wishes from the bride's friends. Emblem of love and duty, the actual tying together of two pieces of cord or ribbon at the marriage ceremony is an old Danish custom, which spread to Holland and England. The knot is also symbolic of oneness, or unity. Today's expression "the knot was tied" means a marriage has taken place.

Next bride. When the bride tosses her bouquet, the woman who catches it will be the next one married, according to another old tradition. She must make a wish for the bride's good fortune, which will come true only if she unties one of the knots in the bouquet ribbons. In France, instead of her bouquet, the bride throws out a fancy garter. Whoever catches it will be married within a year.

Floral shower. In England, Culpeper House, owned by The Society of Herbalists, sells a mixture of dried herbs and spices called "Bless the Bride with natural confetti." Associated with love and happiness, it contains rosebuds (pure and lovely), orange blossoms (bridal festivities), peppermint (warmth of feeling), marjoram (blushes), parsley (festivity), fennel (worthy of all praise), sweet basil (good wishes), mugwort (happiness), rosemary (remembrance), sage (domestic virtue) — "With a touch of cornflower (bachelor's-button) to remind the groom it's all over now!" This colorful throwing mixture is also fragrant.

Angelica. In the seventeenth century, John Parkinson wrote about angelica, the "herb of the angels: "The whole plant, both leafe, roote and seede, is of an excellent comfortable sent, savour and taste." Use *Angelica archangelica*, which is considered "heavenly protection," if available.

Wedding pouch. Make this oldie but goodie by stitching up a small drawstring pouch to pin to the hem of the bridal gown. In the pouch is the bride's insurance policy:

A piece of bread (food)
A scrap of cloth (clothes)
A sliver of wood (shelter)
A dollar bill (money)

(I would also add a sprig of rosemary for luck)

"Herbs of Happiness" (from an Avon tile created in England). "Every flower has its special meaning. Coreopsis is Ever

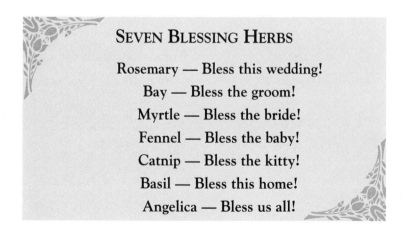

SEVEN BLESSING HERBS

Rosemary — Bless this wedding!
Bay — Bless the groom!
Myrtle — Bless the bride!
Fennel — Bless the baby!
Catnip — Bless the kitty!
Basil — Bless this home!
Angelica — Bless us all!

Cheerful. Larkspur and Yellow Lily are Lighthearted. Chinese Chrysanthemum brings Merriment. Butterfly Orchids express Joy and Lily-of-the-Valley celebrates the Return of Happiness."

Ivy wreath. A wreath of ivy encircles the bride's and groom's dinner plates at the reception to set them apart as guests of great honor and to symbolize "fidelity." Tuck in a few sprigs of sage as well, "to ensure domestic tranquility."

Pikake or Arabian jasmine. *Jasminum sabue* is a small, white, very sweet-smelling flower with nine or ten petals. This wedding flower from Hawaii is used to make lovely pikake leis. *Pikake* means peacock. If you have heavenly perfumed pikake or jasmine flowers, use them in wedding arrangements. If you have enough, string the bride a fragrant lei for "love and luck."

Basil bouquet. There is a legend that if a gentleman accepts from a woman a bouquet of basil — symbol of love, a heavenly scent in many varieties — he will love her forever.

Floral symbols. The Society of American Florists suggests that brides carry lilies-of-the-valley to illustrate the return of happiness; ivy to signify wedded bliss; and orchids to express beauty and refinement. A bit of heather may be added for luck, or asters as the talisman of love.

G. MILEK'S WEDDING HERBS

Globe amaranth	Everlasting love
Sage	Domestic virtue
Thyme	Courage, strength
Nigella	Love-in-the-mist
Lavender	Love, devotion
Rosemary	Remembrance
Marjoram	Joy, happiness
Rose	Love, desire

A Well-Herbed Wedding

The theme for a memorable local wedding centered upon rosemary (for remembrance), gray lavender (for luck), and blue rue (the herb of grace). The bride carried these three herbs with a single large white rose (symbol of love), baby's-breath, and a bit of pearly everlasting (for constancy). The herbs were attached to a muff-sized potpourri bag made of organdy eyelet trimmed with antique beaded lace and satin ribbons to match her off-white gown and supported by ribbons on the back. The fragrant potpourri was a special blend of more symbolic herbs: violet leaves (modesty and simplicity), mullein (once used in love potions), lamb's-ears (for soft caresses), basil (symbol of courtship), sage (for good health and domestic tranquility), linden blossoms (for beauty, grace, and simplicity), along with the thematic lavender, rue, and rosemary, plus rosebuds. It was a sentimental concoction of heavenly fragrance.

Rue

The groomsmen's boutonnieres were made of lavender, rosemary, and rue, which also enhanced the orchid corsages given to the mothers and grandmothers of the bride and groom. Tiny sprigs of the same tri-herbal combination, as well as little sweetheart roses, baby's-breath, and more white pearly everlasting graced the enchanting halo worn by the bride.

Each bridesmaid carried a single long-stemmed pink rose caught with the very same wedding herbs. The bridesmaids also wore headbands similar to the bride's halo.

Two little nieces of the bride carried tussie-mussies of dried rosebuds, fragrant cloves (for dignity), parsley (emblem of victory), and more rosemary glued onto a lacy white paper doily. These were easily made well in advance of the wedding and cherished for years after.

For a touch of whimsy, a pinch of caraway seeds, which are said to have powers of retention, was tucked into the groom's breast pocket (caraway was once believed to keep husbands faithful).

Among the gifts was a basket of herb plants to start a new little kitchen garden. It contained a romanwood plant

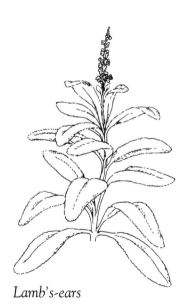

Lamb's-ears

THE LANGUAGE OF HERBS AND FLOWERS

Herbs were used in so many ways down through the centuries that people began to endow them with even greater attributes. Because of their versatility of uses and effect upon people, the mysterious ways in which they can heal, and their magical properties, real or imagined, herbs became a form of communication, an expression of love, victory, or sentiment suitable to all occasions, proper to religious ceremonies and affairs of state.

Herbs became symbolic — and nosegays became the love letters of the day. I've collected a list of some of the symbols and messages that can be conveyed with flowers and herbs; a few more from Gary Milek are listed on page 102.

An interesting combination of five flowers selected from Selam's *Oriental Language of Flowers* would include the following: white lilacs to speak of the first dream of love; dogwood for faith and hope; the daisy, which is a traditional good-luck gift to a woman; pansies for a good-luck gift to a man; and clover blossoms to complete the circle of love and speak of fulfillment and fertility.

Amaranth	Immortality	Cedar	Strength
Ambrosia	Love returned	Celandine	Joys to come
Angelica	Herb of the angels, inspiration, protection	Chrysanthemum	Cheerfulness
		Clover (four-leafed)	Good luck
		Clover (red)	Industry
Apple blossom	Preference	Clover (white)	Promise
Arborvitae	Unchanging friendship; the Tree of Life	Cloves	Dignity
		Coriander	Hidden worth
		Corn	Riches
Artemisias (all varieties)	Everlasting; silvery grays for wreaths	Crocus (spring)	Youthful gladness
		Crocus (fall)	Riches
Basil (sweet)	Good wishes	Cumin	Engagement
Bay laurel	Victory	Daffodil	Regard
Bay wreath	Reward of Merit, triumph, victory	Daisy	Innocence, hope
		Dill	Powerful against witchcraft
Borage	Courage		
Boxwood	Endurance	Dock	Patience
Broom	Neatness	Edelweiss	Devotion, courage
Burnet	For a merry heart	Fennel	Strength
Camomile	Energy in adversity	Fern	Fascination
Caraway	Retention	Flax	Domestic industry

Forget-me-not	Forget-me-not	Nasturtium	Patriotism
Geranium (rose-scented)	Preference	Olive	Peace
		Orange blossoms	Young purity
Gillyflower	Bonds of affection	Oregano	Joy of the mountain
Hawthorne	Hope, charm against witchcraft	Pansy	Thoughts
		Parsley	Festivity
Heliotrope	Devotion, eternal love	Peppermint	Warm feelings
Holly	Foresight	Pinks	Always lovely
Honesty (*Lunaria*)	Money in your pocket	Queen-Anne's-lace	Queen of the meadow
Honeysuckle	Generous and devoted affection	Rose (bridal)	Happy love
		Rose (white)	Youth and beauty, charm, innocence
Hyacinth (white)	Fertility		
Hyssop	Cleanliness	Rose (red)	Desire, love
Iris	A message	Rosemary	Remembrance
Ivy	Fidelity	Rue	Protection from evil
Jasmine (white)	Sweet love	Sage	Domestic virtue, health
Jasmine (yellow)	Passionate love		
Johnny-jump-up	Heart's case	Southernwood (Lad's-love)	Jest, fun
Juniper	Protection		
Lavender	Luck	Strawflowers, statice, and other everlastings	Forever yours
Lemon	Zest		
Lemon balm	Comfort		
Lemon verbena	The herb of Venus, unity		
		Sweet alyssum	Worth beyond beauty
Lilac	Joy of youth	Sweet woodruff	For garlands
Lily-of-the-valley	Sweetness	Thyme	Emblem of courage
Linden blossoms	Conjugal love	Tulip (red)	Declaration of love
Marjoram	Joy	Valerian	Accommodation
Meadowsweet	Once considered the true wedding herb (for strewing)	Vervain	Enchantment
		Violet	Faithfulness
		Wheat	Modesty, prosperity
Mignonette	Quiet sweetness	Willow	Freedom
Mint	Virtue	Wormwood	Absence
Mugwort	Traveler's joy	Yarrow	Everlasting love
Mustard seed	Faith	Zinnia	Missed in absence
Myrtle	True love		

Bertha Reppert, *A Heritage of Herbs*

Basil

(*Artemisia pontica*; for constancy and perseverance), a rosemary plant (sacred to weddings), and a packet of lunaria seeds. Known as *silver dollars* or *moneyplant*, lunaria symbolizes "money in all pockets." It was customarily given to newlyweds to plant in their garden in the belief it would keep the happy household from want. The rosemary plant will prove the test of the marriage for 'tis said that rosemary "grows only where the mistress is master!"

The wedding cake was adorned with asters in the shades of the wedding party gowns, flowers from the bride's grandmother's garden, and snippets of the same lavender, rosemary, and rue. *Hawaiian Wedding Cakes* placed on either side of the traditional tiered cake were decorated with chartreuse lemon balm leaves (for comfort), a perfect complement to the colors and flavors in this delectable recipe.

At the center of the wedding party table was a garland of gray artemisia, silverlike in the moonlight and symbolic of dignity, combined with pink 'Fairy' roses. This was a dried arrangement, which the bride and groom could hang on the door of their new home. The fragrant potpourri bag, too, with all of the wedding herbs, became an heirloom sachet tucked into a bureau drawer as a useful and treasured reminder of this memorable day.

Everyone privileged to attend will long remember the beauty and symbolism of this charming ceremony. The gentle herbs spoke with an eloquence all their own, and the legendary magic of rosemary, lavender, and rue, in company with all the others, will perhaps continue to work their spell on the young couple in mysterious ways. Who can say?

A Second Wedding

A charming couple we know said their vows with herbs at a simple home wedding. At this joyous union of two good-sized families, the bride carried a flat basket in which little herbal nosegays surrounded her larger bouquet, which she treasures as a keepsake. Another similar basket of nosegays was the centerpiece on the buffet table. All together, the baskets contained forty little fragrant tussie-mussies, gay with green, lavender, and yellow ribbon streamers — one for each of the guests and family members to take home as a fragrant symbolic remembrance after the party was over.

The bride chose a sprig of each of the following herbs for every little nosegay. Although the symbolism was handwritten on small white cards by several of the older children; it could be printed professionally:

Mint for Joy
Lavender for Luck
Lemon Balm for Comfort
Southernwood for Fun and Fragrance
A Rose for Love and
Rosemary for Remembrance.

To make the herb bouquets, gather your herbs — mint, lemon balm, roses, southernwood, and so forth — a sprig of each for each bouquet. Condition them (see pages 32–36), and keep them in water as long as possible before putting the little bouquets together. Gather a sprig of each of the herbs together in one informal bunch and secure the stems with twine or a rubber band. Cover the stems with florist's tape or aluminum foil and affix a bow, with or without streamers. Place them in a flat basket. Wrap in plastic and keep under refrigeration until the last possible moment, so they remain well conditioned throughout the festivities.

Candles and Candlelight

A late afternoon or evening wedding in a darkened church or synagogue is magnificent and allows maximum usage of candlelight. Visit the building at the approximate hour of your wedding (taking into account seasonal time changes) to see how many candles are needed for the desired "glow." Be sure to check building regulations on candles before making plans.

Lucky the bride who is wed where the aisle is lighted by tapers in globes. Use long strands of ivy, mint, and artemisia

A SMALL FRAGRANT LAVENDER FAVOR FOR LUCK

1. Make two braids using six spikes of fresh lavender.
2. Form two loops with flower heads hanging down.
3. Tie with bow. (See color photo, page 94.)

HERB CANDLES

♥ To make your own herb-decorated candles, press herbs from the garden for two or three days until flattened but not chip-dry. Melt down used white candle stubs or paraffin, brush the wax on to a large wedding candle, press herbs in place, then cover with another thin coat of melted wax.

♥ You can also affix the wedding announcement into place on a good-sized candle.

tied in place with many velvet bows to decorate the posts and create a picture-perfect scene. If space permits, pedestals with Williamsburg-type chimneys will support lighted candles in the aisle or chancel area.

Chancel candelabras lend themselves to similarly easy ornamentation. Enhance the tall candleholders by adding bows with long streamers. Hang a wreath (see pages 69–72) in front of each candelabra. Tie a simple bunch of herbs on the candlelighter.

In the manner of the Renaissance, bridesmaids can carry lighted tapers. Add bunches of herbs and bows with long streamers. The hall needs to be breeze-free for this one — be sure to have extra matches available, in any case.

The passing of flame stands for unification of families and eternal joys. If the couple chooses, each might take a lighted taper to light a central wedding candle.

Deep windowsills are an especially lovely setting for candle arrangements. In spring, a fat mint-scented candle, yellow taffeta bows, and baby's-breath are a simple, effective decoration. For winter, lay down sprigs of red-berried holly and red velvet bows with spicy candles. Place each arrangement on a 9" x 12" board. (Your friendly lumberyard personnel will cut these for you.) These make the windowsill arrangements portable, so that they can be easily removed to the reception area after the service.

Favors for the Wedding Guests

In some European countries, every guest at the wedding receives a sprig of the true myrtle, symbol of love and devotion. In other countries, rosemary is the treasured remembrance to be given to everyone attending. In Lithuania, where rue is the national emblem, it is distributed at weddings, as it symbolizes good luck and good health.

As guests enter the hall of worship for your wedding, why don't you revive this Old World custom and give each of them a sprig of herbs — for instance, lavender for the bride's family and friends and rosemary for the groom's side. A little boutonniere pin makes it easy to pin these on. Tell the ushers about this charming tradition and which herb is which so they are knowledgeable.

Sweets bags of potpourri (see pages 77–79), tied to a card inscribed with the names of the bride and groom along with

An Herbal Wedding is the essence of romance. The perfumed air, the soft herbal colors, and the ancient symbolism of the plants blend to create a truly magical day. Because of their beautiful scent and symbolic meaning herbs have been used for literally thousands of years in wedding bouquets, garlands, and wreaths. Using herbs in a modern wedding not only ties the bridal couple into ancient tradition but, since each leaf and flower represents a good wish for the newlyweds, also underscores the couple's pledge to each other.

— Betsy Williams,
The Proper Season, Andover, MA

the date, make fragrant and useful favors. Create all-white bags, tied with bows coordinated with the colors of the wedding party, or calico or gingham for a country wedding look.

If your theme is baskets, then little baskets or boxes (see page 68) of homemade mints are a nice touch. *DreaMints* are the hit of every party, especially when done in the wedding bell mold (see recipe on page 153).

PART II

Foods
for Celebrations

Down the primrose path of five decades of matrimony
and cooking, while raising a hungry brood and
entertaining in our various homes, I have collected a
certain number of tried and found-to-be-true recipes.
You may well have your own family favorites,
but let me share some of mine with you.
In all these Reppert recipes the emphasis is on herbs.
Please adjust amounts any way you like and adopt them
as your own. Many of these old favorites are easily made
in advance for gracious, carefree entertaining.
I think you'll find that the collection is the backbone
of a good party file.

Setting a Party Mood

WHEN PLANNING A SHOWER, luncheon, reception, or a simple afternoon tea or open house, think about how you can create a festive party atmosphere. Set your stage by developing an ambiance. Use a theme, a color scheme, lighting, music, and a bower of herbs with flowers. Your well-herbed party will be the talk of the town. Here are some suggestions for background effect:

Entertain with mirrors! For a stunning effect, place food, candles, centerpieces, and pots of herbs on mirrors of assorted sizes and shapes, or on the 12-inch decorator squares sold for walls and ceilings. With everything mirrored dramatically, your party will look twice as good with half the effort.

The charm of lighting. Four vigil light candles placed on a mirror make an inexpensive centerpiece with or without flowers — even for a breakfast party. Place lighted candles in colored glass containers of any kind for a stained-glass-like sparkle. A drop of essential oil in each will perfume the air. Little twinkle lights from Christmas are a striking addition.

I have a talented friend who always likes to entertain in midwinter using one hundred and fifty candles in glasses or glass chimneys throughout the house. It's a fairyland, breathtaking in the quiet of the year.

Scented wash-ups. Borrow an idea from any good Japanese restaurant — serve dampened, heated hand cloths as a wash-up for "finger-lickin'-good" foods. These are easy to prepare: Wet and roll up inexpensive washcloths or terry cloth squares hours in advance of your party. Refrigerate until needed. Then, after the ribs, chicken, or corn-on-the-cob has been served and eaten, pop the attractively arranged basket of damp cloths into your microwave for 2 minutes. Presto! You are passing around toasty-warm wipe-ups grateful guests will appreciate.

Not herbal? Oh, yes. That's your special touch. Add a drop of lemon oil to the water in which you soak the cloths. Or, roll the wet napkins around a sprig of fresh lemon balm from your herb garden.

The food as decoration. The eye feasts first. To have an absolutely smashing party, concentrate your efforts on the presentation of the food you are serving. After laying down your tablecloth, elevate areas of your table or serving area with sturdy cartons and then layer small snowy white cloths, matching napkins, or pieces of colorful fabric over the cartons. Serve your foods on the various levels you have created. Make sure they're all reachable, of course. Here and there, tuck in fruit,

WHEN IT'S YOUR TURN TO ENTERTAIN

Now it's your turn to create a party! After the honeymoon and settling in are over, plan an "at-home" party. An open house, especially over a holiday, is an easy way to return many social obligations in one fell swoop. Pick a day and limit time (say, 4 P.M. to 7 P.M.). Send out herbal invitations and use this book to plan your first party.

Menus and decorations are fun to organize on paper. Put down all your favorite ideas to look over carefully, then decide what's realistic, cross off the impossible, and proceed with your plans. Soft lighting, candles, bowls of potpourri everywhere, background music, flowers, herbs, wedding gifts, and a theme will provide a pleasant environment for your party and ensure success.

This is the perfect opportunity to show the videotape of the wedding and reception. Did you tell the photographer, in advance, to zoom in on your special herbal touches?

vegetables, flowers in water picks, and, naturally, bunches of herbs. In winter, pots of herbs or bunches of supermarket parsley and cress work well; flowering kale is spectacular.

Other focal points. Gather apothecary jars of spices, long cinnamon sticks, and colorful dried flowers to use as table displays, along with country-look animals, your grandmother's antiques, or your favorite small dolls. If you wish, use seasonal items, such as a collection of menorah, Valentine hearts, Easter rabbits, or the family Clauses. The list can go on and on, but I'm sure you get the idea. "Crowded clutter" decoratively arranged is the look you want to achieve. The motto is "and just one more!"

The Bride's Table Napkins

Elegantly flaring linen napkins are the hallmark of the world's most exclusive dining rooms. A well-folded napkin can be a

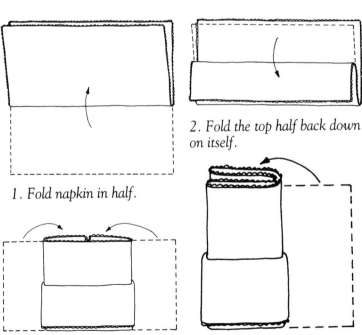

1. Fold napkin in half.

2. Fold the top half back down on itself.

3. Fold a quarter on each side, so that edges meet at the back.

4. Fold in half with back edges to the inside.

5. Place utensils and a sprig of herb into the napkin "pocket" and place in a glass.

SERVE WITH FLAIR!

Even if you haven't run out of time, try this clever, colorful, quick wrap-up for ketchup, mayo, and mustard jars. Place any jar in the center of a napkin or square of material, pull up the four corners, and tie around the jar neck with rubber bands concealed by ribbons. Decoratively swathed in pretty napkins to match your table, they are whisked from pantry to table in a twinkling.

conversation piece, as well as another way to enjoy the presence of herbs.

Choose one of the ways shown on pages 115 and 117 to fold your crisp linens, impeccable white or colored, and place them in tall wine or water goblets (to be filled after seating). Make these yet more impressive by topping them off with a sprig or two of herbs. Place well-conditioned (see pages 32–36) parsley, sage, rosemary, or thyme into a water pick (florists use these to give an individual flower its own supply of water), and tuck them into the folded napkin. Your guests can take them along home.

Each napkin may also be rolled as a scroll, then tied with ribbons in the colors of the wedding party. Catch a perky sprig of rosemary in the bow.

For this use, it might be fun to consider "the guardian herbs," each labeled, of course.

THE GUARDIAN HERBS

Rose	Guardian of True Love
Tansy	Guardian of the Garden
Basil	Guardian of the Loving Heart
Southernwood	Guardian of the Closet
Rosemary	Guardian of Friendship
Sage	Guardian of Health
Bay	Guardian of the House
Parsley	Guardian of the Table
Daisy	Guardian of Innocence and Secrets

In Tudor times, sprigs of gilded rosemary were used at weddings. Gold spray makes this tradition easy to do. It will also serve to preserve the rosemary. Tuck gilded rosemary in your napkins.

NAPKIN FOLDING

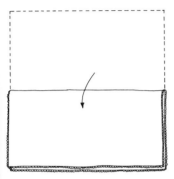

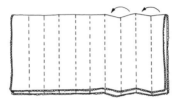

1. Fold a crisp napkin in half.

2. Fan fold back and forth, back and forth.

3. Grasp the bottom and thrust into a goblet.

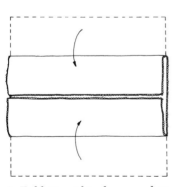

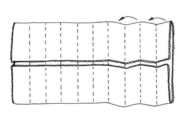

1. Fold ¼ napkin down and ¼ napkin up, meeting in the middle.

2. Fan-fold back and forth.

3. Hold securely, slide on napkin ring or tie with a ribbon before flairing the fans. Add fresh sprigs of herbs at last minute.

CHAPTER 7

Bountiful Buffet Dishes

❧ Salad Banana Splits ❧

Serve this decorative luncheon dish proudly. Easily assembled, it is most attractive.

½ banana for each guest
Ham salad (*with minced parsley*)
Chicken salad (*with minced celery*)
Cottage cheese (*with minced chives*)
Chopped or minced herbs
Red cherries
Green olives
Black olives

1. Purchase long disposable sundae dishes, and place a long sliced half banana in each. Top it with a scoop of ham salad and a scoop of chicken salad on each side of a scoop of cottage cheese.

2. Top each with a garnish of suggested chopped or minced herbs or others such as lovage, mint, burnet, chervil, or basil; cherries; and olives to simulate a banana split. Serve with a deviled egg, a kiwi slice, a pickled beet, and a roll. A simple dessert and beverage complete this fun menu.

❧ Fruited Turkey Salad ❧

3 cups cooked cubed turkey

¾ cup chopped celery

¾ cup halved, seedless red grapes

One 20-ounce can pineapple chunks, drained

One 11-ounce can mandarin oranges, drained

¼ cup chopped pecans

¼ cup "light" mayonnaise

2 tablespoons parsley

⅛ teaspoon salt

2 teaspoons celery seed

1 teaspoon savory

Combine all ingredients, and chill well before serving. Serve in lettuce cups. Makes 6 servings

❧ Superb Main Course Chicken Salad ❧

If the season permits, consider serving this delicious chicken salad in tulip cups or daylily blossoms. Stew your chickens a day or two before the party.

3-pound whole chicken

4 quarts water

6 stalks celery, chopped

½ cup fresh parsley

4 tablespoons chopped onion

1 teaspoon dried tarragon

Pinch dried rosemary (4 leaves)

Other favorite seasonings, such as lovage, burnet, saffron, lemon thyme

4 cups finely minced celery

4 cups mayonnaise

1. In a large soup pot, combine first eight ingredients, and cook until meat leaves the bone, about 40 to 50 minutes. Cool. Debone and cut chicken into bite-sized pieces. Reserve any extra chicken and the broth for other use.

2. Combine 4 cups chicken pieces, 4 cups celery, and mayonnaise. Makes 12 servings.

To this basic chicken salad, add one or more of the following, your choice:

black olives, diced red apple, green peas, chunked pineapple, hard-boiled eggs, slivered almonds, other nuts (peanuts are good), green grapes, avocado pieces, mandarin oranges, pimiento, green bell pepper, red rose petals, water chestnuts

Italian Wedding Soup

3-pound whole frying chicken

6 quarts water

1 small bay leaf

1 small whole onion

3 stalks celery, chopped

1½ pounds escarole or endive

3 tablespoons all-purpose flour, to thicken

Dash salt

1 teaspoon grated cheese (Romano or Parmesan)

1 egg, slightly beaten

Meatballs

¾–1 pound ground beef

1 egg

½ cup bread crumbs

3 tablespoons grated cheese (Romano or Parmesan)

1 tablespoon crushed dried mint leaves

1 teaspoon salt

⅛ teaspoon freshly ground black pepper

Dash garlic powder

Chopped fresh parsley, optional

Milk

1. In a 7- or 8-quart pot, place chicken, water, bay leaf, and onion. Cook 45 to 60 minutes, or until meat is soft, skimming off foam as chicken cooks. Remove chicken from cooking stock and let cool. Debone and shred.

2. Add celery and meatballs to soup stock. **To make meatballs:** Combine meatball ingredients, and add enough milk to form tiny meatballs the size of marbles. Let meatballs cook, and again remove any foam that appears.

3. Wash, drain, and cut up escarole, and add to soup. Return the shredded chicken to the soup.

4. Mix together flour, dash of salt, 1 teaspoon grated cheese, and slightly beaten egg. Make into a thin paste (the consistency of pancake batter) and drizzle over boiling soup. You may have to add a little water or milk to paste to get it to drizzle into soup. Makes 20 to 30 servings.

✂ Sharon's Easy and Delicious Ham Casserole ✂

2 cups uncooked macaroni

2 cups evaporated milk

2 cups grated sharp cheddar cheese

1½ cups ham cubes

Two 10¾-ounce cans cream of golden
mushroom soup, undiluted

1 medium onion, diced

1. Preheat oven to 350°F.

2. Mix all the ingredients in a bowl. Pour
into a greased casserole dish. Bake 1 hour.

Optional: Add 3 hard-boiled eggs, diced
during the last 10 minutes of baking time.
Serves 10 to 12.

✂ Upside Down Ham 'n' Swiss Pie ✂

2 cups cut-up, fully cooked, smoked ham

1 cup shredded natural Swiss cheese (about 4
ounces)

⅓ cup chopped green onions or chopped
onion

¼ cup chopped parsley, oregano, and/or dill

4 eggs

2 cups milk

1 cup packaged baking mix

¼ teaspoon salt, if desired

⅛ teaspoon freshly ground black pepper

1. Preheat oven to 400°F.

2. Grease 10" x 1½" pie plate. Sprinkle ham,
cheese, and onions in plate. Beat remaining ingredients until smooth, 15 seconds
in blender on high or 1 minute with hand
beater.

3. Pour into plate. Bake until golden brown,
and knife inserted in center comes out
clean, 35 to 40 minutes. Cool 5 minutes.
Makes 6 servings.

✂ Lemon-Mint Rice ✂

1 cup white rice

¼ cup butter or margarine

1 teaspoon finely chopped fresh parsley

¼ teaspoon each grated lemon peel and dried
mint leaves

Cook rice according to package directions.
Toss with butter, parsley, lemon peel, and
dried mint. Makes 4 servings.

❧ Three-Cheese Broccoli Bake ❧

1 cup packaged baking mix

¼ cup finely chopped onion

¼ cup milk

2 eggs

½ cup grated Parmesan cheese

One 12-ounce carton creamed cottage cheese

One 10-ounce package frozen chopped broccoli, thawed and drained

4 ounces Monterey Jack cheese, cut into ½" cubes

2 cloves garlic, crushed

2 eggs

Pinch each of rosemary, basil, and/or marjoram

1. Preheat oven to 375°F.

2. Grease rectangular baking dish, 12" x 7½" x 2". Combine baking mix, onion, milk, and 2 eggs. Beat vigorously 20 strokes. Spread in dish.

3. Mix remaining ingredients, and spoon evenly over batter in dish. Bake until set, about 30 minutes. Cool 5 minutes. Makes 6 to 8 servings.

❧ Tuna Mousse ❧

1 can tomato soup, undiluted

One 8-ounce package cream cheese

2 envelopes unflavored gelatin, dissolved in ½ cup cold water, then heated on low

One 13-ounce can water-packed solid white tuna

¾ cup finely chopped celery

¼ cup chopped scallion

½ cup chopped red onion

2 heaping tablespoons white horseradish

1 teaspoon Worcestershire sauce

1 cup mayonnaise

Black pepper and Tabasco sauce to taste

1. Heat soup. Add cheese in small pieces, and mix well with a whisk until dissolved.

2. Add gelatin, mix in well, and take off the burner. Add tuna (completely minced and drained) and remaining ingredients. Mix well.

3. Pour into lightly buttered mold. (Takes a few hours to gel. Use a pretty mold and this will crown your party. Makes 8 servings.

Tomato-Rose Hip Aspic

3 envelopes unflavored gelatin
2½ cups tomato juice, divided
½ cup rose hips
3 cups water
1 tablespoon fresh lemon juice
Lettuce, for garnish

Rose hips

1. Soften gelatin in 1 cup tomato juice for 5 minutes.

2. Combine rose hips and water in a saucepan. Bring to a boil, and simmer gently for 15 minutes. Strain, discarding rose hips, and return liquid to saucepan. Add softened gelatin.

3. Place on low heat, stirring until gelatin is dissolved. Add lemon juice and remaining tomato juice. Mix well. Turn into 6-cup mold, which has been dipped in cold water just before, and chill until set. Unmold by dipping the mold into warm water.

Note: Up to 1 cup of chopped vegetables may be added to the aspic. If using vegetables, before turning mixture into prepared mold, chill mixture until slightly thickened, stirring occasionally. Then stir in chopped vegetables. Turn into mold, and chill until set. Garnish with real roses. (Color photo, page 93.)

❧ Apricot Gelatin Salad ❧

Two 0.35-ounce packages apricot gelatin

3¾ cups boiling water

2 large bananas, thinly sliced

1 20-ounce can crushed pineapple, drained; reserve juice

1 tablespoon minced lemon balm or lemon verbena

Topping

½ cup granulated sugar

1 egg

2 tablespoons all-purpose flour

1 tablespoon butter

½ cup pineapple juice

One 3-ounce package cream cheese

1 package whipped topping mix

2 tablespoons chopped chocolate mint, for garnish

1. Mix together gelatin and water, and put into a 9" x 13" pan. Let soft set.

2. Add the bananas, pineapple, and lemon balm or lemon verbena.

3. Cook topping ingredients — sugar, egg, flour, butter, and juice — on medium heat until thickened. Add cream cheese, and blend and cool.

4. Make whipped topping as directed on package and add to topping. Spread on gelatin and fruit salad. Garnish with chocolate mint. Makes 15 servings.

❧ Superbowl Coleslaw ❧

2 eggs

Red beet juice

1 medium head white cabbage

Dressing

¼ cup vegetable oil

⅛ cup fresh lemon juice

½ teaspoon prepared mustard

Dash paprika

¼ teaspoon celery salt

⅛ cup mayonnaise

Salt to taste

Freshly ground black pepper to taste

1. Hard-cook eggs. Peel and soak in beet juice until whites turn a gorgeous color. (These can be purchased at some delicatessens.) Grate or chop eggs.

2. Cut cabbage in half, and soak in salty ice water for several hours. Shake off excess water, and cut in half again. Shred as thinly as possible. Combine eggs and shredded cabbage.

3. Mix together all dressing ingredients, and pour over coleslaw. Toss well. Refrigerate until ready to serve. Makes 10 to 12 servings.

❧ Toasted Sesame Salad ❧

½ cup sesame seeds

1 tablespoon butter

¼ cup grated Parmesan cheese

1 cup sour cream

½ cup mayonnaise

1 tablespoon tarragon vinegar

1 tablespoon granulated sugar

1 teaspoon salt

1 clove garlic, minced

2 heads Bibb or leaf lettuce

1 medium cucumber, thinly sliced

½ medium green bell pepper, chopped

2 green onions, sliced

1 medium carrot, pared and cut into thin strips

Tomato slices or wedges, for garnish

1. In a small skillet, sauté seeds in butter until lightly browned. Remove from heat, and add Parmesan cheese. Set aside.

2. In a small bowl, blend sour cream with mayonnaise. Add vinegar, sugar, salt, and garlic.

3. Tear lettuce into bite-sized pieces and place them in a salad bowl. Add cucumber, bell pepper, onions, and carrot. Toss with half of sesame seed mixture. Sprinkle remaining seeds on top. If desired, garnish with tomato slices or wedges. Pour sour cream mixture over all. Makes 6 to 9 servings.

❧ Pretty Party Sandwich Loaf ❧

1 cup butter or margarine, softened

1 cup grated American cheese (¼ pound)

1 cup grated Port Salut cheese (¼ pound)

One 8-ounce package cream cheese, softened

2 ounces Bleu cheese

2 teaspoons ground paprika

1 teaspoon Worcestershire sauce

½ cup sour cream

½ cup chopped, pimiento-stuffed olives

4 hard-cooked eggs, chopped

1 teaspoon ground curry

Two 4½-ounce cans deviled ham

¼ cup heavy cream

3-pound loaf of bread (Pullman-style), unsliced

Pimiento strips

Whole pimiento-stuffed olives

Stems of parsley, chervil, burnet, and basil, for garnish

1. Combine ½ cup of the butter with cheeses, paprika, Worcestershire sauce, and sour cream. Beat until well blended. Take out 1½ cups cheese mixture, and stir in chopped olives; reserve for filling.

2. Mix together chopped eggs, remaining ½ cup butter and curry; reserve for filling.

3. Mix deviled ham with heavy cream; reserve for filling.

4. Remove crusts from Pullman loaf and slice bread lengthwise into 4 long slices. Spread ham filling on bottom layer of bread, top with second layer, and spread with olive-cheese filling. Top with third layer and spread with egg filling. Top with fourth layer and frost entire loaf with remaining cheese mixture.

5. Run tines of fork along loaf for bark-like appearance. Decorate top of loaf with strips of pimiento and whole olives. Chill several hours or overnight. Garnish with a wreath of parsley, chervil, burnet, and basil. Slice with sharp knife to serve. This 16" loaf makes 16 or more servings.

"Stratified" Dishes

Entice your guests with a menu of "stratified" foods, such as *Swiss Cheese Strata*, *Fruit Strata*, and *Salad Strata*. These recipes are easily prepared twenty-four hours in advance, allowing you the freedom to enjoy your party and your guests. Just add some crackers to go with the salad and cookies to go with the fruit and serve a hot or cold beverage. Your reputation as a hostess is assured with these recipes, which are gorgeous to look at as well as delicious to eat.

℀ Swiss Cheese Strata ℀

1 loaf French bread, cut into 1-inch cubes (about 8 cups)

One 11-ounce can cheddar cheese soup, undiluted

2 cups shredded Swiss cheese

4 eggs, slightly beaten

1 soup can water

1 tablespoon fresh oregano (or 1 teaspoon dried)

⅓ cup sauterne or other dry white wine

1. In a buttered 2-quart shallow baking dish (12" x 8" x 2") arrange bread cubes.

2. In a bowl, combine remaining ingredients and pour over bread. Cover. Refrigerate 6 hours or overnight.

3. Preheat oven to 350°F. Bake, uncovered, for 30 minutes or until hot. Makes 6 to 8 servings.

℀ Fruit Strata ℀

1 cup melon balls or cubes

1 cup blueberries

1 cup peach slices

1 cup strawberries or raspberries

Mint sprigs, pineapple sage, lemon verbena and/or rose geranium leaves

½ cup low-fat pineapple yogurt

1. Layer colorful fresh fruits in a large glass bowl (my favorite is a tall-stemmed compote). Lay down a few herbs and spread yogurt on top. Cover and chill for at least 2 hours (can be made 24 hours in advance).

2. Garnish with additional berries and the rest of the herbs (kept fresh in a glass of water in the refrigerator). Makes 6 to 8 servings. (Color photo, page 94.)

❧ Salad Strata ❧

1 large head lettuce

Several stalks celery

2 medium green bell peppers

1 medium sweet onion

One 10-ounce package frozen peas

1 cup sour cream

1 cup mayonnaise

2 tablespoons granulated sugar

¼ pound cheddar cheese, grated

1 cup minced fresh herbs, such as parsley, mint, chervil, burnet, lovage

1. Quarter, wash, drain, cut fine, and pat dry lettuce. Wash and scrape celery, and cut into small pieces (about 2 cups). Wash, core, and cut bell peppers into strips. Cut onion into thin rings or chop.

2. Cook peas (no butter) in a little salted water. Drain.

3. Place in layers in a glass bowl in order given, including herbs, saving half of lettuce as top layers. Mix sour cream and mayonnaise together, and spread over salad. Do not stir. Sprinkle sugar over salad and cover all with grated cheese. Cover bowl with plastic. Refrigerate 24 hours or at least 8 hours until cold and crisp. Makes 8 generous servings.

Salad burnet

Wedding and Party Cakes

THE WEDDING CAKE ITSELF has had quite a long and interesting history. At the Roman *confarreatio*, a form of marriage ceremony, the couple ate a cake made of salt, water, and flour, and the bride carried three wheat ears as a symbol of plenty or fruitfulness. In the Middle Ages, in a variation of this custom, wheat grains were thrown after the bride. Later, grains were baked into biscuits, which were broken over the bride's head.

In England, it was the custom to bring small, richly spiced buns to a wedding. These were piled into a tall mound over which the bride and groom were to kiss. If they succeeded, prosperity was assured them. But the mounds were cumbersome, and, it is said, a French cook conceived the idea of icing them into a solid whole. This, then, was the origin of the wedding cake. Traditionally, the bride herself cuts the first slice as a security that no outside force shall cut into her happiness.

✒ Minga's Wedding Cake ✑

Minga's memorable wedding, which featured garden flowers galore, was crowned with the best cake I've ever eaten. If you don't want to make it yourself, assemble all the ingredients and ask your best local baker to do it for you. It's worth any effort. **The Bride's Cake** *and* **Groom's Cake** *are combined to make one impressive three-tiered cake. Both may be made ahead and stored for several days, wrapped separately in foil; they may also be frozen. When ready to use, put together in graduated layers with* **Minga's Wedding Cake Icing** *(which should be made in two batches).*

Bride's Cake

8 egg whites; reserve yolks for *Groom's Cake*

2 cups granulated sugar

1 cup butter

1 teaspoon pure lemon extract

1 teaspoon pure vanilla extract

3½ cups all-purpose flour

4 teaspoons baking powder

1 cup light cream

½ pound grated coconut

¼ pound candied orange peel, finely chopped

½ pound chopped almonds

1. Preheat oven to 300°F.

2. Beat egg whites until stiff. Beat in 1 cup sugar, 2 tablespoons at a time, and set aside.

3. Cream the butter and the remaining cup of sugar. Add the flavorings.

4. Mix and sift dry ingredients, and add to the butter and sugar mixture alternately with the cream. Mix in fruit and nuts. Fold in beaten egg whites.

5. Butter and flour three pans, 12, 9, and 6 inches in diameter. Bake in a slow oven 300°–325° for 1 to 1½ hours, depending on pan size. Cool in pans 10 minutes, then remove from pans, and put on cake racks to cool completely.

WEDDING CAKE PROPHESIES

Sometimes a ring is baked into the cake, so that the person who finds it may be the next one to marry. Small pieces of the cake are regularly distributed to young, unmarried women, who take them home and place them under their pillows — it being presumed that one's future husband will thus reveal himself in a dream.

Groom's Cake

½ cup granulated sugar

1½ cups packed brown sugar

1 cup butter

8 egg yolks

3 cups all-purpose flour

1 teaspoon baking soda

Generous ½ teaspoon each ground cloves,
    nutmeg, cinnamon, and allspice

1 cup whiskey

1 pound seedless raisins

½ pound dried currants

¼ pound candied orange peel, finely chopped

¼ pound chopped nuts

1. Preheat oven to 300°F.

2. Cream sugars and butter, then add egg yolks, and beat well. Add flour mixed with baking soda and spices alternately with whiskey. Mix in fruit and nuts.

3. Butter and flour three pans, 12, 9, and 6 inches in diameter. Bake in a slow oven 300°–325° for 1 to 1½ hours, depending on pan size. Cool in pans 10 minutes, then remove from pans and put on cake racks to cool completely.

The Icing

1 cup soft butter

½ teaspoon salt

3 teaspoons pure vanilla extract

6 pounds sifted confectioners' sugar

8–10 egg whites

½ cup light cream

1. In a large bowl, cream and beat butter until light. Add salt and vanilla, and mix in. Gradually add sugar and egg whites alternately, and beat well. Add enough cream for a good spreading consistency. Do not tint *Wedding Cake Icing*.

2. Cover a round piece of white cardboard with a large lace paper doily. Protect this with strips of waxed paper, which may be pulled out when finished decorating. Place the 12-inch *Groom's Cake* on this, frost thinly, and top with the 12-inch *Bride's Cake*.

3. Cut a 9-inch round of white cardboard and center on the lower cakes. Place 9-inch *Groom's Cake* on this, frost thinly, and top with 9-inch *Bride's Cake*.

4. Do the same with the 6-inch layers.

5. Frost the whole cake. Pipe rosettes of

icing around edges of each layer. Place a small nosegay of fresh flowers in the center of the 6-inch layer.

To cut: Cut first (bottom) layer all the way around, then the second layer around. Cut first layer around again. Save the top for the bride. Then cut rest of cake. Makes 68 wedding cake slices.

CUTTING TIERED CAKES

To cut round tiers, move in 2 inches from the tier's outer edge, and cut a circle. Then, slice 1-inch pieces within the circle. Now move in another 2 inches, cut another circle, and slice 1-inch pieces. Continue in this manner until the tier is completely cut. The center core of each tier and the small top tier can be cut into halves, fourths, sixths, and eighths, depending on size.

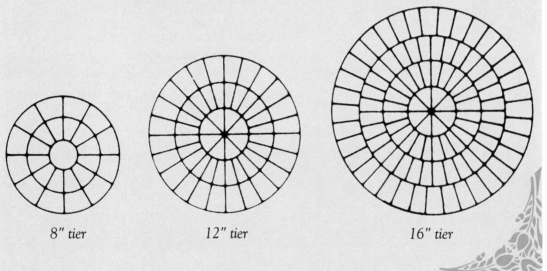

8" tier　　　　*12" tier*　　　　*16" tier*

Nancy's Carrot Wedding Cake

1½ cups vegetable oil

1½ cups granulated sugar

4 eggs, well beaten

3 cups grated carrots

2 cups unbleached all-purpose flour

½ teaspoon salt

2 teaspoons baking soda

2 teaspoons ground cinnamon

2 teaspoons ground allspice (or 1 tablespoon apple pie spice)

1 cup chopped pecans

1 cup raisins

1 teaspoon pure vanilla extract

Frosting

½ cup butter, at room temperature

One 8-ounce package cream cheese, softened

4 cups confectioners' sugar

1 teaspoon pure vanilla extract

1 cup chopped nuts (added to mixture or sprinkled on top)

1. Preheat oven to 325°F.

2. Cream oil and sugar, then add eggs and carrots. Mix well.

3. Mix together dried ingredients, and add to the carrot mixture, a small amount at a time, beating well. Then add nuts, raisins, and vanilla.

4. Pour into a 9" x 13" greased and sugared pan, and bake 1 hour. Cool before frosting.

5. For frosting, cream butter and cheese. Add sugar and vanilla, and beat. Frost. Keep cake refrigerated, but serve at room temperature. Makes 12 to 15 servings.

HAVE A BIG HEART

If you do not have heart-shaped cake pans, use any favorite family recipe or mix to make a large romantic party cake. Baked in a square and a round pan, 8 inches, 9 inches, or larger. Cut the round cake in half and place as shown. Decorate with icing or fresh flowers and herbs.

Place large cakes on wooden boards, cut to size and covered with aluminum foil. For a dramatic presentation, make several large heart-shaped cakes.

8" round cake pan

8" square cake pan

❧ Mexican Wedding Cake ❧

1 cup chopped pecans

One 20-ounce can crushed pineapple,
   undrained

2 cups granulated sugar

2 cups all-purpose flour

1 teaspoon baking soda

½ teaspoon salt

2 teaspoons pure vanilla extract

2 eggs

Icing

One 8-ounce package cream cheese

½ cup margarine

1½ cups confectioners' sugar

2 teaspoons pure vanilla extract

1. Preheat oven to 350°F.

2. Combine all cake ingredients in a large bowl. Mix well.

3. Pour into a greased and floured 9" x 13" pan. Bake 45 to 50 minutes.

4. Mix all icing ingredients together, and spread on cooled cake. Makes 12 to 15 servings.

❧ Italian Love Cake ❧

1 angel food cake

½ cup amaretto

1 pint pistachio ice cream

1 pint strawberry ice cream

2 cups heavy cream (1 pint)

One 6-ounce package semisweet chocolate
   morsels

1. Using a sawing motion with a sharp serrated knife, cut the cake into three layers. Sprinkle each layer with 2 tablespoons of amaretto. Place one layer on a serving platter.

2. Cut ice cream into slices and place pistachio ice cream on bottom layer. Top with second cake layer and a layer of strawberry ice cream. Top with third cake layer. Place in freezer.

3. In a bowl, mix heavy cream and remaining amaretto, and beat until very thick. Frost the sides and top of the cake, and replace in freezer.

4. Melt chocolate on very low heat until smooth. Spread chocolate in a ¼-inch

thick layer on aluminum foil, and chill until chocolate hardens.

5. With a small cookie cutter, cut hearts out of chocolate, and place on top of cake. Freeze cake until ready to serve. Makes one 9-inch cake, or 10 to 12 servings. (Color photo, page 94.)

❧ Cool and Minty Bridal Cake ❧

One 14-ounce can sweetened condensed milk (not evaporated milk)

2 teaspoons pure peppermint extract

8 drops green food coloring

2 cups (1 pint) whipping cream, whipped (*do not use nondairy whipped topping*)

One 18½-ounce package white cake mix

Green crème de menthe

One 8-ounce container frozen nondairy whipped topping, thawed

Mint leaves, for garnish

1. In a large bowl, mix sweetened condensed milk, peppermint extract, and food coloring. Fold in whipped cream.

2. To make ice cream layer, pour this mixture into aluminum-foil-lined 9-inch round layer cake pan. Cover. Freeze 6 hours or until firm.

3. Prepare and bake cake mix as package directs for two 9-inch round layers. Remove from pan and cool completely.

4. With table fork, poke holes in layers 1 inch apart halfway through each layer. Drizzle small amounts of crème de menthe in holes.

5. Place cake layer on serving plate. Top with ice cream layer, then second cake layer. Frost with nondairy whipped topping, and decorate with mint leaves. Keep in the freezer until the day of the party, but allow time to soften **slightly** before cutting. Makes one 9-inch cake, or 10 to 12 servings.

❧ Spicy Gingerbread ❧

¾ cup vegetable shortening

¾ cup packed brown sugar

2 eggs

¾ cup dark molasses

2½ cups all-purpose flour

2 teaspoons baking powder

2 teaspoons ground ginger

1 teaspoon freshly ground black pepper

1½ teaspoons ground cinnamon

½ teaspoon ground cloves

½ teaspoon ground nutmeg

½ teaspoon baking soda

½ teaspoon salt

1 cup boiling water

1. Preheat oven to 350°F.

2. Cream shortening and brown sugar. Add eggs, beating after each one. Add molasses and mix well.

3. Stir all dry ingredients together with a wire whisk. Add dry mixture alternately with water to the molasses mixture.

4. Pour mixture into well-greased and floured 9-inch square pan. Bake 45–50 minutes or until center springs back when touched with fingertip. Serve warm or cold. *Tangy Lemon Sauce* is delicious on it, or grind 3 tablespoons sweet cicely leaves and 1 cup confectioners' sugar in a mortar with pestle. Dust it through a paper doily for a lacy pattern on your gingerbread. Serve on a lacy sweet cicely leaf. Makes 9 to 12 servings.

❧ Tangy Lemon Sauce ❧

1 cup granulated sugar

3 tablespoons cornstarch

2 cups water

2 egg yolks, beaten

1½ cups fresh lemon juice

1 tablespoon grated lemon peel

1 tablespoon minced lemon verbena

2 tablespoons soft butter

Lemon geranium leaves, for garnish

1. Combine sugar and cornstarch in a saucepan. Gradually add water, blending until smooth. Cook on medium heat, stirring constantly until mixture becomes thick and clear. Remove from heat.

2. Stir small amount of hot mixture into egg yolks, and then add egg yolks to the hot mixture in the saucepan. Cook 2 minutes. Add lemon juice, lemon peel, lemon verbena, and butter. Blend well. Serve warm or cool. Garnish with lemon geranium leaves. Makes 2¾ cups.

❧ Poppyseed Pound Cake ❧

Poppyseeds are just what you'd think — seeds of that beautiful flower. We import almost all of our poppyseeds from the Netherlands, Australia, and Turkey, but you can use the poppyseeds from your garden. Poppyseeds have been a favored ingredient since ancient Greek and Roman times, but nobody has ever topped the ways in which central Europeans use these tiny blue seeds.

1 cup poppyseeds

⅓ cup honey

¼ cup water

1 cup butter or margarine, softened

1½ cups granulated sugar

4 eggs, separated

1 cup sour cream

1 teaspoon pure vanilla extract

2½ cups unsifted all-purpose flour

1 teaspoon baking soda

1 teaspoon salt

1 cup confectioners' sugar

4 teaspoons cold water

1. Preheat oven to 350°F.

2. In a small saucepan, cook poppyseeds with honey and water for 5 minutes. Cool.

3. In a large mixing bowl, cream butter with sugar until light and fluffy. Stir in cooled poppyseed mixture.

4. Add egg yolks, one at a time, beating well after each addition. Blend in sour cream and vanilla extract.

5. Sift together flour, soda, and salt. Gradually add to poppyseed mixture, beating well after each addition.

6. Beat egg whites until stiff peaks form. Fold into batter. Pour batter into lightly greased and floured 10-inch tube pan. Bake until done, about 1 hour and 15 minutes.

7. Cool in pan on a rack for 5 minutes. Remove cake from pan to a rack. Cool completely.

8. Blend confectioners' sugar with cold water until smooth. Spoon over cake. Makes 1 large cake, or about 15 servings.

❧ Quick-and-Easy Poppyseed Cake ❧

½ cup poppyseeds

1⅓ cups water

One 18½-ounce package white cake mix

One 1-ounce box instant vanilla pudding mix, prepared as directed

One 8½-ounce package fluffy white frosting mix

1. Soak poppyseeds in the 1⅓ cups water at least 1 hour.

2. Prepare batter as directed on package, **except** substitute poppyseed mixture for water. Bake cake in two round layer pans, 8" or 9". Cool.

3. Fill layers with 1 cup of pudding, and spread remaining pudding on top.

4. Prepare frosting as directed on package. Frost sides and top of cake. Refrigerate leftover cake. Makes one 8- or 9-inch cake, or 8 to 10 servings.

❧ Hawaiian Wedding Cake ❧

This is exquisite on a lei of lemon balm.

One 18½-ounce package yellow cake mix

1 cup milk

One 2.1-ounce package instant vanilla pudding

One 8-ounce package cream cheese, softened

One 20-ounce can crushed pineapple

One 3½-cup package whipped topping mix

One 3½-ounce can flaked coconut

1. Bake cake according to package directions in a 13" x 9" pan. Let cool.

2. Mix together milk, contents of pudding mix package, and cream cheese. Spread over cooled cake.

CHAPTER 9

Romantic Cookies

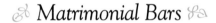

Matrimonial Bars

1¾ cups all-purpose flour

½ teaspoon baking soda

¾ cup butter or margarine, softened

1 cup packed brown sugar

1½ cups quick oats

One 8-ounce jar strawberry or raspberry jam (1 cup)

1. Preheat oven to 400°F.

2. Stir together flour and soda. Set aside.

3. In a medium-sized bowl, cream butter and sugar until light and fluffy. Stir in flour mixture until well blended. Blend in oats with fingers or a wooden spoon. Dough will be crumbly.

4. Press half the dough into a greased 13" x 9" pan. Spread with jam. Crumble remaining dough over top, and pat lightly to cover.

5. Bake 20 to 25 minutes or until lightly browned. While warm, cut into 2" x 1½" bars, and remove from pan. Serve warm or cooled. Store airtight in a cool place. Makes 30 bars.

Crisp Caraway Cookies

1⅔ cups all-purpose flour

1 teaspoon baking powder

¼ teaspoon baking soda

¼ teaspoon salt

2 teaspoons caraway seeds

½ cup butter or margarine, softened

⅔ cup granulated sugar

2 eggs

½ teaspoon pure vanilla extract

1. Preheat oven to 375°F.

2. Mix together flour, baking powder, baking soda, salt, and caraway seeds. Set aside.

3. Cream butter and sugar until fluffy. Add eggs and vanilla, and beat well. Stir in flour mixture. Wrap dough in plastic wrap, and chill several hours or overnight or until firm enough to roll (dough will still be rather soft).

4. Working with one-fourth of the dough at a time (keep remainder refrigerated), roll very thin on a floured surface (easiest with pastry cloth and rolling pin cover). Cut with floured 3-inch round cutter. Put on ungreased cookie sheets.

5. Bake on top rack of oven 8 to 10 minutes, watching closely. Remove to wire rack to cool. Repeat. Store airtight or freeze. Makes about 48. (Color photo, page 91.)

❧ Mexican Wedding Cookies ❧

1 cup butter or margarine, softened

½ cup confectioners' sugar, plus extra for dusting

1 teaspoon pure vanilla extract

¼ teaspoon salt

2 cups all-purpose flour

1. Preheat oven to 375°F.

2. In a medium-sized bowl, cream butter, ½ cup confectioners' sugar, vanilla, and salt until fluffy. Stir in flour until well blended. Chill 30 minutes or until firm enough to handle.

3. Shape into 1-inch balls. Place 1 inch apart on ungreased cookie sheet. Bake 12 to 15 minutes or until lightly golden. Remove to wire rack (close together), and while still warm, dust heavily with confectioners' sugar. Cool.

4. Store airtight in cool, dry place. Before serving, dust cookies with additional confectioners' sugar. Makes 48.

❧ Melissa's Lemon Whippersnaps ❧

One 18½-ounce package lemon cake mix

2 cups (4½ ounces) frozen whipped topping, thawed

3 teaspoons dried lemon balm

1 egg

½ cup sifted confectioners' sugar

1. Preheat oven to 350°F. Grease cookie sheets.

2. Combine cake mix, whipped topping, lemon balm, and egg in a large bowl. Stir until well mixed.

3. Drop by teaspoons into confectioners' sugar, roll to coat. Place 1½ inches apart on cookie sheet.

4. Bake 10 to 15 minutes or until light golden brown. Remove from cookie sheet. Cool. Makes about 4 dozen.

Lemon-Caraway Refrigerator Cookies

2⅓ cups all-purpose flour
½ teaspoon baking soda
½ cup butter or margarine, softened
1 cup granulated sugar
1 egg
2 tablespoons fresh lemon juice
1 teaspoon grated lemon peel
1¼ teaspoons caraway seeds
Colored sugar, optional

1. Preheat oven to 375°F.

2. Stir together flour and baking soda. Set aside.

3. In a medium-sized bowl, cream butter and sugar. Beat in egg until light and fluffy. Beat in lemon juice, peel, and caraway seeds until blended. Stir in flour mixture just until well blended.

4. Shape into a roll about 2 inches thick. Wrap. Chill 1 hour.

5. Remove roll from refrigerator. If it is flat on bottom, roll on counter so cookies will be round when cut. Chill several hours more or overnight.

6. With very sharp knife, cut into ¼-inch slices. Place on greased cookie sheets, and sprinkle with colored sugar.

7. Bake 10 minutes or until lightly browned around edges. Remove immediately to wire racks to cool. Store loosely covered in cool, dry place. Makes 36.

❧ English Tassies ❧

Shells

¼ pound butter

One small 3-ounce package cream cheese

1 cup sifted all-purpose flour

Filling

¾ to 1 cup chopped pecans; reserve ¼ cup
for top

2 tablespoons melted butter

2 eggs

Pinch salt

1½ cups packed light brown sugar

A few drops of pure vanilla extract

1. Preheat oven to 350°F.

2. Cream together butter and cream cheese. Add flour. Place in refrigerator to chill, as it will handle better.

3. Divide into balls (20–25 or more). Press into small muffin tins to form shells.

4. Mix together all filling ingredients and beat until blended. Fill shells and sprinkle reserved nuts on top.

5. Bake 35 minutes. Take out of pans while slightly warm. Makes 20–25.

❧ English Tarts ❧

Filling

2 cups granulated sugar

1 pound raisins

1 cup butter

4 eggs, beaten

1 cup chopped nuts

1 teaspoon ground cinnamon

Pastry

1¼ cups all-purpose flour

⅓ cup plus 1 tablespoon
vegetable shortening

¼ teaspoon salt

3–4 tablespoons milk

Johnny-jump-ups,
for garnish

Johnny-jump-ups

1. Preheat oven to 400°F.

2. Mix together all filling ingredients, and cook until thickened, stirring to prevent scorching. Cool.

3. Mix together pastry ingredients in blender. Roll out and cut into 3-inch circles. Place pastry circles in smallest muffin tins and fill with filling.

4. Bake 15 minutes at 400°. Reduce to 350° and bake until crust is brown, about 15–20 minutes. Cool. Garnish with Johnny-jump-ups. Makes 24 tarts.

CHAPTER 10

Festive Fruits

FRESH FRUIT USED LAVISHLY is nothing short of spectacular and always appropriate. Here are some recipes to begin, make, or end the meal with our favorite fruits.

Katy's Blueberry Soup

1 cup water

½ cup granulated sugar

1 cinnamon stick

2 tablespoons cornstarch

¼ cup water

One 6-ounce can frozen lemonade concentrate (thawed)

1 quart buttermilk

1 quart blueberries

One 8-ounce carton blueberry yogurt

Whipped cream and mint sprigs, for garnish

1. Boil the 1 cup water with the sugar and cinnamon stick until sugar is dissolved. Mix the cornstarch with the ¼ cup water, and add to boiling mixture. Boil until clear.

2. Remove from heat and add the lemonade concentrate, buttermilk, blueberries (smash some of the blueberries so they release their color). Blend in yogurt. Stir soup with the cinnamon stick, or remove the stick before serving. Top with a dollop of whipped cream and a sprig of mint. Makes 12 one-cup servings.

Fruit Salads

Mixed fruit bowls are always lovely to look at and refreshing to eat. Choose the freshest fruits of the season, wash them carefully, peel and section as required, and serve in your most beautiful bowls with one of the following dressings.

Mint Dressing for Fruit

½ cup granulated sugar

1½ cups vegetable oil

1 cup fresh lemon juice

1½ teaspoons salt

½ teaspoon pure mint extract (or one 8-inch long sprig fresh mint leaves — see note)

Note: If using mint leaves, place leaves in covered blender container. Blend sugar, oil, lemon juice, salt, and mint until mixture is smooth. Pour into bottle. Cover and refrigerate at least 12 hours for flavor to develop. Serve as above.

Salad Dressing #1

One 6-ounce can frozen lemonade concentrate, thawed

One 6-ounce can frozen orange juice concentrate, thawed

1 cup vegetable oil

1 tablespoon honey

½ tablespoon Worcestershire sauce

Dash cayenne pepper

6 tablespoons finely diced candied ginger

Salad Dressing #2

1 cup orange juice

6 tablespoons honey

4 tablespoons chopped sweet cicely leaves

Into covered blender container, place sugar, oil, lemon juice, salt, and mint extract. Blend at medium speed until mixture is smooth. Pour dressing into a 1-quart bottle or container. Cover and refrigerate. Shake before using on fruit salad. Makes 3½ cups. This recipe may be made early in the day or up to 1 month ahead.

English mint

Salad Dressing #1

Blend all ingredients, except ginger, in a blender, or shake vigorously in a tightly covered jar. Add ginger. Keeps well refrigerated. Shake before serving. Makes 2 cups.

Salad Dressing #2

Mix together all ingredients, and simmer 2 minutes to blend. Pour over fruits in salad and chill before serving. Makes 1½ cups.

❧ Melissa's Ambrosia ❧

6 large sweet navel oranges

One 20-ounce can pineapple slices, drained

One 3½-ounce can flaked coconut

½ cup lemon balm leaves

¼ cup granulated sugar

⅔ cup sweet sherry

1. Peel, thinly slice crosswise, and seed oranges. Arrange three oranges in a large shallow dessert bowl. Alternate with half the pineapple slices, and sprinkle with half the coconut, lemon balm, and sugar.

2. Repeat using remaining ingredients.

3. Pour sherry evenly over all. Cover bowl with plastic wrap and chill until serving time. Makes 6 to 8 servings.

❧ Wedding Fruit Salad ❧

One 20-ounce can pineapple chunks in own juice, well-drained

2 medium bananas, peeled and thinly sliced

2 medium oranges, peeled and sectioned

3 kiwis, peeled and thinly sliced

1 pint strawberries, washed and hulled

1 cup melon balls

Lettuce leaves, optional

1 tablespoon chopped lemon verbena leaves

Dressing

1 clove garlic, peeled and slightly crushed

5 tablespoons fresh lemon juice

1 cup cranberry juice cocktail

1 tablespoon light corn syrup or honey

½ teaspoon salt

¼ teaspoon ground paprika

1. **To prepare dressing:** Let garlic stand in lemon juice at room temperature for at least 2 hours. Remove. Add remaining ingredients and blend well. Chill. Shake well before pouring over prepared fruit.

2. Arrange pineapple chunks, banana slices, orange sections, kiwi slices, whole strawberries, and melon balls in lettuce-lined salad bowl. Sprinkle with chopped verbena. Makes 10 to 12 servings.

❧ Skewers of Beautiful Fruits ❧

Using 8-inch bamboo skewers, available at any kitchen shop, line up chunks of pineapple, green grapes, maraschino cherries, a mushroom, a square of cheese, a thick slice of banana (rolled in lemon juice to keep from browning), and a segment of mandarin orange. This pretty array is both side dish and/or garnish.

❧ Fruit Cloud ❧

A picture-perfect fruit dessert to steal the show.

2 egg whites, at room temperature

½ tablespoon cream of tartar

⅛ teaspoon salt

¼ teaspoon pure vanilla extract

⅔ cup granulated sugar

½ cup heavy cream

1 tablespoon confectioners' sugar

1½ cups fruits of your choice

One 2.1-ounce package lemon chiffon pie filling, prepared according to package directions

Additional fruit and whipped cream (optional)

Sprigs of lemon balm and lemon verbena, for garnish (pansies, too, are spritely, if available)

Lemon verbena

1. Preheat oven to 275°F.

2. Beat together the egg whites, cream of tartar, salt, and vanilla extract until mixture holds its peaks. Slowly add sugar while continuing to beat until stiff and glossy. On greased brown paper on a cookie sheet, make an 8-inch meringue shell with a bottom crust ¼ inch thick and sides about 2 inches high. Bake 1 hour or until crisp and cream-colored. Cool. Remove to a flat dish.

3. Whip the cream and confectioners' sugar then spread in bottom of meringue shell.

4. One hour before serving time, add the fruits, cut into small pieces, to prepared pie filling. Pour fruit mixture over cream in meringue shell.

5. At serving time, top with more fruit and more whipped cream, if desired. Garnish with sprigs of lemon balm and lemon verbena. Makes 8 servings.

✂ Lime-Mint Sherbet ✄

12 sprigs fresh mint
2 cups water
¾ cup granulated sugar
½ cup light corn syrup
2 teaspoons grated lime rind
½ cup fresh lime juice
Green food coloring (optional)
2 egg whites, stiffly beaten

1. Set freezer control for fast freezing.

2. Pick mint leaves from stems and chop.

3. In a saucepan, combine mint leaves, water, and sugar. Bring to a boil, stirring until sugar dissolves. Cool and strain.

4. Add corn syrup, lime rind, and juice. Tint with coloring. Freeze until firm.

5. Break up mixture, and beat until it is a smooth mush. Fold in egg whites, and freeze until firm. Makes 2 pints.

✂ Grapes Royale ✄

Stir 1 cup sour cream into 4 cups stemmed, washed, seedless grapes (about 2 pounds) in a medium-sized bowl. Chill until serving time. Spoon into a serving bowl or individual dessert dishes, and sprinkle lightly with 2 tablespoons brown sugar. Garnish with mint. Makes 6 servings.

✂ Melissa's Lemon Gelatin ✄

Make a tea of lemon balm leaves steeped in boiling water (see *Lemon Balm Jelly* on page 154) for 10 minutes. Use the strained liquid to make lemon gelatin. Capture a sweet woodruff whorled leaf on top.

Sweet woodruff

For your dieting friends, serve low-calorie foods attractively and creatively. Sugar-free gelatin sparkles like a jewel when served in tall wine glasses.

✃ Spiced Iced Oranges ✄

16 amaretto cookies

8 large oranges, peeled

¼ teaspoon ground cinnamon

½ teaspoon ground cloves

⅓ cup granulated sugar

1 cup orange liqueur

Sprigs of mint, for garnish

1. Crush cookies.

2. Thinly slice oranges, toss with spices and sugar, and freeze. Add any juice to liqueur and reserve.

3. To serve oranges, pile frozen segments in elegant stemmed glasses. Sprinkle with liqueur and top with crushed cookies. Garnish with mint. Makes 10 to 12 servings.

Note: If you add coconut, it's "Ambrosia."

✃ Summer Dessert Platter ✄

¼ small watermelon, cut into 1-inch pieces

1 pound fresh pineapple spears or unsweetened chunks, canned

3 large oranges, peeled and sliced into rounds

1 pint strawberries, washed and hulled

4 medium peaches, pared, sliced, and dipped into lemon juice

1 pint blueberries, washed

1 pound seedless white grapes, washed and divided into small bunches

1 pound seedless red grapes, washed and divided into small bunches

4 medium bananas, peeled, cut into rounds, and dipped into lemon juice

1 pint lime sherbet

1. Arrange watermelon wedges in the center of a large platter, around a glass dish (to hold sherbet). Select four or more of the suggested fruits. Prepare them and arrange them in groups around the tray.

2. Add the bananas and peaches (if used) just before serving, as well as placing the sherbet in the dish. Garnish lavishly with mint, lemon verbena, parsley, burnet, lovage, and edible flowers (see chapter 14). Makes 6 servings.

❧ Fabulous Fruit Compote ❧

One 17-ounce can pitted dark sweet cherries

One 16-ounce can sliced peaches, drained

One 12-ounce package dried apricots

1 tablespoon grated orange peel

1 tablespoon grated lemon peel

½ cup orange juice

¼ cup fresh lemon juice

½ teaspoon ground cardamom

¾ cup packed light brown sugar

Sour cream or sweetened whipped cream

1. Preheat oven to 350°F.

2. Turn cherries and their liquid into a 2-quart casserole. Add peaches, apricots, orange and lemon peels, and juices. Sprinkle with cardamom and brown sugar.

3. Bake, covered, 1½ hours. Let cool slightly. Refrigerate, covered, several hours or overnight or until well chilled. Serve with sour cream or sweetened whipped cream. Makes 6 to 8 servings.

❧ Minted Grapes ❧

2 pounds green seedless grapes in small bunches, 3 to 5 grapes to a bunch

2 egg whites, beaten until frothy (can be colored green)

1 cup granulated sugar

2 peppermint tea bags

Wash and pat dry grapes. Dip in frothy egg whites. Place on waxed paper, and cover completely with sugar mixed with the contents of the dried peppermint tea. Allow to dry in refrigerator until serving time. Makes 40 to 50 servings of 3 to 4 clustered grapes per serving.

If you're planning a wedding party, make your weight-watching guests happy by serving food and drinks that are high in taste appeal, but low in calories, such as chicken breasts, fruit salads, and diet drinks.

Sometimes it seems as though absolutely everybody is on a diet — a fact that can put a crimp in the menu planning of any hostess. When you can't fight the diet craze, join it by planning party menus with a light touch. Yet another time when herbs can make the difference!

CHAPTER 11

Desserts and Sweetmeats

❧ Melissa's Lemon Pudding Dessert ❧

Make one day ahead.

1½ cups all-purpose flour

1½ sticks margarine, softened

¾ cup chopped pecans

One 16-ounce package cream cheese, softened

4 tablespoons finely minced dried lemon balm

1 cup confectioners' sugar

One 9-ounce carton nondairy whipped topping; reserve half for topping

Three 2.1-ounce packages lemon instant pudding

4½ cups milk

Chopped nuts, for garnish

1. Preheat oven to 325°F.

2. Mix together flour, margarine, and pecans, and pat firmly into the bottom of a 9" x 13" pan.

3. Bake about 25–30 minutes. Cool.

4. Mix together cream cheese, lemon balm, confectioners' sugar, and ½ the whipped topping with electric mixer, and spread over crust.

5. Mix pudding and milk until pudding is dissolved, and spread over cream cheese mixture. Let set until firm.

6. Spread remaining whipped topping on top, and sprinkle with chopped nuts. Makes 12 to 15 servings.

✤ Sinfully Sensational English Trifle ✤

This is an elegant dessert.

1 pint strawberries

1 two-layer sponge cake

6 tablespoons strawberry jam

½ pound macaroons, broken into pieces

1 cup sherry

1 cup custard or pudding

½ pint heavy cream

1. Line a crystal trifle bowl with strawberries that have been sliced and lightly sugared. Place one layer of sponge cake in the bowl, and spread strawberry jam over it. Cover with second layer of sponge cake. Add a layer of macaroons.

2. Pour sherry over contents of bowl. Pour custard over all, and chill until set.

3. Shortly before serving, whip the cream. Top with sweetened whipped cream and Alpine strawberries from your herb garden. Makes 12 to 15 servings.

✤ Parting Party Parcels ✤

In India, similar after-dinner treats are served as an aid to digestion and to cleanse the palate. Keep the exquisite little packets on ice — with a smattering of rose petals. How elegant!

2 cardamom seeds

A few each of dill, anise, and fennel seeds

1 piece crystallized ginger

2 candied mint leaves or mint candies

4 peanuts

Pinch coconut (may be tinted)

Grape or maple leaf, or a corn husk

Cinnamon stick (optional)

Parcel out each of the ingredients onto a grape or maple leaf or a corn husk. Secure with whole cloves, or tie each packet with string. Bows and a cinnamon stick are optional. Makes 1 packet — make as many as you need for your party.

❧ Rosemary's DreaMints ❧

Every party and wedding reception needs DreaMints, always a hit. Make them at your leisure; have them ready when you need them. There are many little soft molds available (rose-, leaf-, heart-, and bell-shaped molds are wedding favorites). If molds are not available, make small balls, then flatten them into patties. This is a project even small children can enjoy. You can make the DreaMints in the wedding colors, if you wish. They freeze well.

Two 1-pound boxes confectioners' sugar

One 8-ounce package cream cheese, softened

A few drops of favorite flavoring (peppermint, lemon, and so on)

A few drops of appropriate food coloring (pink for peppermint, yellow for lemon, and so on)

Granulated sugar

1. Add confectioners' sugar to cream cheese a little at a time, blending well. Add flavoring and food coloring, and continue kneading until well mixed, creamy, and colorful.

2. Roll into small balls, then roll in a saucer of granulated sugar.

3. Press into mint molds, then pop out. Arrange on flat plates. Makes 150 to 200 mints, depending on the size of the molds (leaves and hearts are smaller and thus make more).

Peppermint

❧ Lemon Balm Jelly ❧

3½ cups water

A large handful of lemon balm (about 1 cup)

4 cups granulated sugar

One 1¾-ounce box fruit pectin

Juice of ½ lemon

½ capful of yellow food coloring

1. **To make the infusion or tea:** Boil the water and pour it over the lemon balm. Steep until cool, and strain. Measure 3 cups of the infusion.

2. Combine it with the remaining ingredients. Bring to a vigorous boil that cannot be stirred down, and boil for 1 minute. Pour into sterilized glass jars and use paraffin to seal. (Color photo, page 93.)

❧ Nancy's Best Spiced Nuts ❧

Use any kind of nuts, such as peanuts, pecans, walnuts, hazelnuts, or cashews.

1 egg white

1 teaspoon water

2 cups nuts

½ cup granulated sugar

¾ teaspoon ground cinnamon

¼ teaspoon ground cloves

¼ teaspoon ground allspice

¼ teaspoon salt

1. Preheat oven to 240°F.

2. Mix together egg white and water, and beat until frothy. Stir in nuts until well coated. Combine sugar, spices, and salt, and sprinkle over nuts. Mix well.

3. Spread coated nuts on an oiled shallow pan. Bake about 1 hour, stirring every 20 minutes until coating hardens. Store nuts in tightly covered containers. They may also be frozen. Makes ½ pound of delicious nuts.

CHAPTER 12

To Toast
the Bride and Groom

⚘ Hot Mulled Cider ⚘

6 medium oranges

Whole cloves (about 12 dozen)

2 gallons apple cider

1 teaspoon ground cloves, cinnamon, allspice,
and/or ginger

1 teaspoon freshly grated nutmeg

Long and short cinnamon sticks, for stirrers

*". . . and so they lived
happily ever after."*

1. Preheat oven to 150°F.

2. Stick the oranges full of cloves (about 2
dozen to each orange). Bake in oven until
soft and juicy, about 20 minutes. (If you
wish, you can do this step in the microwave. Watch the oranges carefully; it will
take only about 1 minute.)

3. Place oranges in slow cooker, and pour 2
gallons apple cider over them. Stir in the
spices.

4. Stir with long cinnamon sticks. Keep
heated while serving. Serve with short cinnamon sticks. Makes 36 servings.

❧ *Percolator Punch* ❧

Fill your percolator basket with cinnamon sticks, sugar, and spices — and you have the tasty beginnings of a hot festive punch. This nonalcoholic spiced punch is especially appropriate for winter weddings, church socials, and as an "extra" beverage when liquor is served.

2½ cups pineapple juice

1¼ cups water

2 cups cranberry juice

1 tablespoon whole cloves

½ tablespoon whole allspice

3 sticks cinnamon

¼ teaspoon salt

½ cup firmly packed brown sugar

Pour pineapple juice, water, and cranberry juice into bottom of 8- to 12-cup automatic coffee maker. Place remaining ingredients in basket. Set heat control on "strong" and complete perking cycle. Hold on "mild" setting. Serve hot in mugs or heatproof punch cups. Makes 8 to 12 servings.

Drink to me only with thine eyes,
And I will pledge with mine;
Or leave a kiss but in the cup,
And I'll not look for wine.

— Ben Jonson, "To Celia"

WARMING MIXER

For an evening treat on a cool day, mix equal parts of strong coffee and hot chocolate. Then top with whipped cream and a tiny sprinkle of freshly grated nutmeg. Serve with crisp cookies. Allow 1 cup per person.

✂ Five Herb Teas ✂

Any time is the perfect time for a pot of good herb tea. Iced or steamy hot, depending upon the weather, herbs can lift your spirits, satisfy inner longings, and taste delicious to boot. A host of wonderful flavors may be found fresh from your herb patch or in teabags on market shelves. Here are just a few suggestions. Oh yes, sometimes we offer guests a basket of assorted herbal tea bags. Then it's their tantalizing decision.

To make a flavorful brew, use 1 teaspoon or teabag of the herb to 1 cup freshly drawn, briskly boiling water. Steep 5 to 10 minutes, then strain to serve. Herb tea is usually pale in color. Tasting is the only way to determine strength.

Peppermint

The number-one herb tea that everyone loves! Symbolizing virtue, mint was considered so valuable at one time, it was used for titheing. It has a cool, mouth-cleansing effect and is an aid to digestion.

Hibiscus

This rosy red drink has a citrus-tart tang. Children are especially fond of this red thirst-quenching beverage. In Africa, it is called *carcadeeh*, which means *beverage that brings health*.

Rose Hip Blend

The rose, which symbolizes love, has been eaten for centuries. Rose water, rose wine, and rosepetal preserves are still enjoyed today. The seedpods of the rose — called *rose hips* — contain an enormous amount of valuable vitamin C. Rose hip tea has a delectable, fruit-and-wine-like taste. It is especially good mixed with hibiscus tea.

♥

By those we love —
— May we be loved

Camomile

Camomile flowers brew into a delicately flavored, sunny yellow drink. Symbolizing "energy in adversity," camomile is an ancient herb dating back to the Egyptians. It is the tea once given to Peter Rabbit to ward off a possible cold after he raided Mr. McGregor's cabbage patch.

Four-Herb Tea Blend

Combine equal amounts of rose hips, hibiscus, peppermint, and camomile to make a delightful blend of beneficial and ancient herbs that will be enjoyed by young and old alike. It has a full-bodied flavor and a lovely wine-red color that makes a delectable, fragrant drink.

German camomile

❧ Royal Wedding Punch ❧

We first devised this wonderful recipe to celebrate the nation's bicentennial. We served it as "Patriot's Punch." No matter the occasion, it is always a hit. It may be served with or without alcohol.

1 quart boiling water

5 teaspoons whole mint leaves (fresh or dried)

3 teaspoons whole rosemary (fresh or dried)

2 teaspoons whole sage (fresh or dried)

1 cup granulated sugar

One 6-ounce can frozen lemonade concentrate, undiluted

4 teaspoons instant tea

2 gallons cold water

1 quart whiskey (optional)

Lemon slices and whole cloves

Pour boiling water over all herbs, and let steep 10 minutes. Strain and add remaining ingredients. Stir thoroughly. Serve with lemon slices stuck with whole cloves. Makes thirty 3-ounce servings.

*This is a golden opportunity to serve the same beverage with or without alcohol.

❧ Carolynn's Reception Punch ❧

One 6-ounce can frozen lemonade concentrate, undiluted

One 48-ounce can pineapple juice, chilled

2 bottles sauterne, chilled

One large bottle champagne (magnum)

Orange slices, maraschino cherries, Alpine strawberries, herbs, for garnish

1. Combine frozen lemonade concentrate and pineapple juice in a punch bowl. Add one tray ice cubes or a block of ice made of lemonade.

2. Just before serving, pour in wines (or sparkling water for a nonalcoholic version). Garnish with oranges, cherries, strawberries, and herbs. Makes forty-five 3-ounce servings.

To Health!
To life!
To love!

✂ Sangria ❧

1 gallon sweet red wine

1 gallon diet lemon-lime soda

Juice of 1 lemon

Ice

Fresh fruits (sliced apples, oranges, and lots
of sliced lemons)

Mix all ingredients together, and serve.
Makes thirty 3-ounce servings.

✂ Rosemary Wedding Wine ❧

1 gallon pale-dry sherry or white wine
(sauterne or chablis)

6 sprigs fresh rosemary (or 2 tablespoons
dried rosemary in a muslin bag)

Steep rosemary in wine for 1 week before the
wedding. Strain, chill, and serve.

Note: For a nonalcoholic version, use 1
gallon apple juice instead of wine. Makes
fifteen 3-ounce servings.

✂ Rosey Rosé Punch ❧

6 fifths rosé wine, chilled

2 quarts cranapple juice

1 pint rose water

2 cups light corn syrup

1 cup fresh lemon juice

Ice ring, with roses

Lemon slices and fresh rose petals, for garnish

Stir together all ingredients, and blend well.
Pour over ice ring filled with roses in a large
punch bowl. Add lemon slices, and float rose
petals to garnish. Makes seventy-five 3-ounce
servings.

TIPS FOR MAKING A ROSE-FILLED ICE RING

To embed roses (or any other edible herbs or flowers; see chapter 14) in ice cubes
or an ice ring, fill the container only half full of water and arrange the flowers as
desired. Freeze until water is completely frozen. Fill container to the top with ice
water and immediately replace container in freezer.

❧ Rosé Punch ❧

6 fifths rosé wine, chilled

2 quarts clear apple juice

2 cups light corn syrup

1 cup fresh lemon juice

Stir together all ingredients and blend well. Garnish with lemon slices and lemon balm. Makes seventy-five 3-ounce servings.

❧ Gazpacho Fizz ❧

4 tablespoons tomato purée

1 scallion bulb, with a bit of green

½ medium stalk celery, roughly chopped

1 tablespoon fresh lemon juice

¼ teaspoon celery seed

6½ ounces cold sparkling mineral water

Stick of cucumber or leafy, hollow stalk of lovage, for garnish

1. In a blender, combine all ingredients and blend to a fine purée. Chill thoroughly.

2. Pour into stemmed glass. Stir in mineral water, and garnish with a cucumber stick or a stalk of lovage. Makes 1 serving.

Lovage

*"A toast to love and laughter
— Another to happily ever after!"*

❧ Melissa's Punch ❧

This is an excellent punch, with or without alcohol. It is nice to use two matching punch bowls, one with just the ingredients listed and the other with a litre of sherry instead of the second quart of water. Pour over ice, and garnish with lemon balm and strawberries. A ruffle of lemon balm around the base of the punch bowl is lovely.

¼ cup dried lemon balm leaves (or a handful fresh from the garden)

2 quarts water

One 6-ounce can frozen lemonade concentrate, undiluted

One 8-ounce can crushed pineapple

16 ounces frozen strawberries

2 or 3 quarts ginger ale

1. **To make the lemon balm (Melissa) tea:** Steep the lemon balm leaves in 1 quart briskly boiling water. Steep 10–15 minutes and strain. Add second quart of water.

2. Blend together lemonade concentrate, pineapple, and strawberries (reserve a few strawberries to float as garnish). Combine the tea and fruit mixture.

3. Before serving, add the ginger ale, and garnish with strawberries. Makes 20 to 24 servings.

❧ Melissa's Lemon Balm Lemonade ❧

1½ cups granulated sugar or to taste

1 cup water

Grated peel of 2 lemons

1½ cups fresh lemon juice

3 cups lemon balm tea (see *Melissa's Punch*)

Crushed ice

Slices of lemon

Sprigs of lemon balm

1. Combine sugar, water, and grated peel in a saucepan. Bring to a boil and simmer for 5 minutes. Strain and chill.

2. Stir in lemon juice and lemon balm tea. Pour into a covered jar, and refrigerate until ready to use.

3. Fill tall glasses with crushed ice and 2 lemon slices each. Add ¼ cup of the chilled lemon mixture, and fill with ice water. Mix, and garnish each glass with a lemon balm sprig. Makes 10 to 12 servings.

❧ White Grape Juice Punch ❧

3 quarts white grape juice

3 quarts ginger ale

Grated rind of 6 lemons

1½ cups water

1½ cups mixed fruit (pineapple, red or green seeded grapes, orange sections, and strawberries)

¾ cup frozen lemonade concentrate, thawed

½ cup frozen orange juice concentrate, thawed

12–16 drops pure peppermint extract

Mint sprigs for garnish

1. Chill grape juice and ginger ale. Put lemon rind and water into a saucepan, and boil, uncovered, until liquid is reduced to half. Strain and chill.

2. Put any combination of fruits you like into a punch bowl. Pour grape juice and ginger ale over fruits. Add lemon and orange juice concentrates, extract, and the chilled lemon rind liquid. Add ice. Decorate with sprigs of mint. Makes 40 servings (7 quarts).

❧ Colleen's Slushie ❧

Because of the alcohol, this mixture never freezes to a very hard state, so it can be made weeks in advance and kept in the freezer.

One 6-ounce can frozen orange juice concentrate, prepared

One 6-ounce can frozen lemonade concentrate, prepared

One 6-ounce can whiskey sour mix

Sugar, optional, to taste

1 litre diet lemon-lime soda

1. Blend all ingredients, except diet soda, and freeze.

2. Scoop into glasses. Add diet soda to fill glass. Makes twenty 4-ounce servings.

♥

Here's to my mother-in-law's daughter,
And here's to her father-in-law's son;
And here's to the vows we've just taken,
And the life we've just begun!

CHAPTER 13

Herbal Dips, Nibbles, and Tidbits

❧ Hot Olive-Cheese Dip ❧

One 7½-ounce can minced clams
Two 8-ounce jars processed cheese spread
1 cup (¼ pound) grated cheese, any kind
½ cup mayonnaise
⅛ teaspoon garlic powder
1 teaspoon Worcestershire sauce
1 cup chopped, pimiento-stuffed olives

1. Preheat oven to 400°F.

2. Drain liquid from clams and reserve ¼ cup. Combine reserved clam liquid, clams, and remaining ingredients in a 1½-quart casserole. Bake 10 minutes. Stir and bake 5 to 10 minutes longer or until bubbly.

3. If desired, transfer to chafing dish, and serve in miniature patty shells, or serve as dip for corn and potato chips. Makes 5 cups.

For neat and tidy plates, make your finicky guests happy by serving small individual cups of herb dip. Easy to handle at buffets, they allow for individual convenience and neatness. Garnish each cuplet with an herb, alike or different. Serve with crisp veggies or crackers.

❧ Liptauer Cheese ❧

1 teaspoon ground mustard
2 tablespoons warm water
½ cup butter or margarine, softened
One 8-ounce package cream cheese, softened
1 tablespoon minced onion
3 anchovy fillets, minced
1 tablespoon capers, minced
1 tablespoon caraway seeds
Few twists freshly ground black pepper

1. In a cup, combine mustard and warm water. Let the mixture stand 10 minutes to develop flavor.

2. In a small mixing bowl, beat butter with electric mixer until soft. Add cream cheese, blending well.

3. Add mustard mixture along with remaining ingredients. Mix thoroughly. Serve as a spread with crackers. Makes 2 cups.

❧ Tish's Crab Dip ❧

To vary this already excellent, easy dip, add finely chopped spring onions or green bell pepper, or both.

One 3-ounce package cream cheese
⅓ cup mayonnaise
3 tablespoons ketchup
1 tablespoon grated onion (best if fresh; can substitute onion powder not onion salt)
One 6⅛-ounce can crabmeat, rinsed and drained

Mix together all ingredients, except sour cream. (Add 1 heaping teaspoon or more sour cream to achieve a thinner consistency.) Let sit for 2 hours in refrigerator before serving. Makes 1 cup.

❧ Mega-Easy Dip ❧

1 jar French dressing
One 8-ounce package cream cheese

Mix the dressing into the cream cheese until it tastes good! Makes 2 cups.

❧ Susanna's Conversation Piece ❧

A chocolate sundae look-alike that is actually a tasty spread.

One 8-ounce package cream cheese, whipped
¾ cup steak sauce

Put whipped cheese into a shallow serving dish, and liberally pour steak sauce over it. Serve with crackers.

❧ Dilled Salmon Dip ❧

A Russian classic — and easy!

One 16-ounce can red salmon
½ cup sliced green onions
¼ cup chopped fresh dill
1 cup sour cream
2 tablespoons white wine
⅛ teaspoon freshly ground
    black pepper

1. Drain red salmon well. Remove skin and bones, and discard. Flake fish into a small bowl. Add green onions and chopped dill. Toss to mix.

2. Heat sour cream in top of chafing dish over flame until warm. Stir in salmon mixture, white wine, and black pepper.

3. Place boiling water in bottom of chafing dish; set dish over flame. Put top over bottom to keep dip hot for serving. Makes 3 cups.

❧ Dilly Dip ❧

1 cup sour cream
⅔ cup mayonnaise
A little grated onion
1 tablespoon celery seeds
1 tablespoon dill weed

Combine all ingredients. Mix well. Makes about 2 cups.

Dill

❧ Marjorie's Pineapple Dip ❧

One 16-ounce package cream cheese, softened
8 ounces crushed pineapple, drained
2 tablespoons chopped green onions, include tops
½ cup chopped green bell pepper
2 tablespoons seasoned salt
2 cups chopped pecans
½ fresh pineapple (optional)

1. Combine cheese and pineapple with an electric mixer. Stir in onions, bell pepper, salt, and half of the pecans.

2. Roll into a ball or a log, or fill a scooped out fresh pineapple half. Press remaining pecans into top. Makes 2 cups.

❧ Rosemary House Party Sandwich Spread ❧

¼ pound dried beef, soaked and drained

¼ pound sharp cheese

¼ medium green bell pepper

1 small onion, chopped

1 egg

1 cup tomato purée or soup

1 teaspoon basil

½ teaspoon oregano

Grind together dried beef, cheese, bell pepper, and onion. Add egg, purée, and herbs. Cook slowly 5 minutes. Makes 2½ cups or enough for 10 to 12 sandwiches.

❧ Yogurt Herb Dip with Crudités ❧

2 teaspoons instant dried onion

2 tablespoons dried parsley flakes

4 tablespoons dried dill weed

¼ cup warm water

2 cups plain yogurt

½ cup mayonnaise

1½ teaspoons seasoned salt

1 teaspoon fresh lemon juice

Soften onion, parsley, and dill weed in the warm water for 10 minutes. Combine all ingredients. Chill several hours before serving. Makes 5 cups.

A BOUQUET OF CRUDITÉS

Make your crisp-fresh vegetable platter as colorful as possible, with any or all of the following:

raw carrot sticks	cherry tomatoes	radishes	string beans
celery sticks	cucumber spears	broccoli buds	asparagus spears
cauliflowerettes	eggplant fingers	whole green beans	summer squash chunks
zucchini slices	raw mushrooms	sweet red pepper strips	snow peas

❧ Parsley Butter ❧

2 sticks very soft butter

¾ cup finely cut fresh parsley

¼ teaspoon grated onion (or more if you like)

Combine all ingredients. Place in refrigerator overnight. Remove from the refrigerator to soften before using spread. Can be kept for weeks, covered. Makes 1½ cups.

❧ Sage Sandwich Spread ❧

One 8-ounce package cream cheese

½ pound butter

1 tablespoon onion juice

1 tablespoon fresh sage (or 1 teaspoon dried)

1 tablespoon celery salt

1 tablespoon fresh lemon juice

Beat all ingredients together until light and fluffy. Serve with hot biscuits or thin brown bread. Makes 1½ cups.

❧ Cheese Bread ❧

½ cup butter

1⅔ cups granulated sugar; reserve ¼ cup for top

2 eggs

1 cup milk

2 cups all-purpose flour

1 teaspoon dried oregano

½ teaspoon salt

3 teaspoons baking powder

One 8-ounce package cream cheese, cubed

½ cup chopped walnuts

¼ cup fresh orange juice

2 tablespoons orange rind

1. Preheat oven to 350°F.

2. Cream butter with sugar. Add eggs, milk, flour, oregano, salt, and baking powder. Alternately fold in cubed cheese and walnuts.

3. Bake 40–50 minutes.

4. While bread is baking, mix together orange juice, reserved ¼ cup sugar, and rind. Pour over bread after removing from oven, while hot. Makes 1 loaf.

❧ Herbwiches ❧

If you don't have access to an herb garden, use a bunch of parsley and celery or watercress tops from the supermarket with dried culinary herbs in any combination. These pretty open-faced sandwiches will be delicious, decorative, and well received. (Color photo, page 93.)

10–12 red radishes, grated

3 medium cucumbers, scrubbed and grated

2 generous handfuls culinary herbs (parsley, chives, mints, garlic chives, lemon balm, sage, burnet, tarragon, lovage, thyme, marjoram, basil, savory, rosemary — whatever you have)

2 loaves small party rye, round and thin

One 8-ounce package cream cheese, softened

½ cup mayonnaise

Garlic chives

1. Grate unpeeled radishes and cucumber. Drain.

2. Finely chop, snip, or mince the herbs (easily done in a food processor). Mix with grated vegetables.

3. Combine cream cheese and mayonnaise.

4. Spread party rounds with cream cheese mixture, and top with a generous mound of herb mixture. Serve on a large tray, garnished with additional herbs. Makes 60 to 80 servings.

❧ Midget Poppyseed Triangles ❧

A slick trick with a knife turns refrigerated rolls into these one-bite delights.

1 package refrigerated flaky rolls

2 tablespoons butter or margarine, melted

1 tablespoon poppyseeds

1. Preheat oven to 375°F.

2. Separate the rolls. Cut each roll into quarters. Place quarters, 1 inch apart, on an ungreased cookie sheet.

3. Brush with melted butter or margarine, and sprinkle with poppyseeds. Bake about 10 minutes. Serve hot. Makes 4 dozen.

✂ Sesame Seed Cheddar Sticks ✂

Sprinkle sesame seeds into a skillet and heat them over moderate heat until golden before stirring them into a mixture or showering them over food. These nibblers are especially nice with drinks, soup, or salad.

1½ cups unsifted all-purpose flour

½ teaspoon salt

2 tablespoons sesame seeds

1 cup shredded sharp cheddar cheese (4 ounces)

½ cup butter or margarine

3 tablespoons Worcestershire sauce

2 teaspoons cold water

1. Preheat oven to 450°F.

2. In a mixing bowl, combine flour, salt, and sesame seeds. Cut in cheese and butter with pastry blender or two knives until crumbly.

3. Sprinkle with Worcestershire sauce and water. Stir together with fork until mixture clings to side of bowl. Shape into a ball; handle lightly.

4. On a lightly floured board, roll out dough ¼" thick. Cut into 3" x ½" strips; a zigzag cutter lends a nice touch.

5. Place on ungreased baking sheets and bake 8 to 10 minutes or until golden. Remove to wire racks. Cool. Makes 3 dozen.

✂ Buttery Parmesan Crescents with Herb Butter ✂

Two 8-ounce packages refrigerated crescent dinner rolls

½ cup (1 stick) butter, melted (or use *Parsley Butter* on page 167)

½ cup grated Parmesan cheese

1. Preheat oven to 375°F.

2. Unroll dough. Brush each piece generously with melted butter, and sprinkle with Parmesan cheese. Roll up as package directs.

3. Place on unbuttered baking sheet. Drizzle remaining butter over crescents and sprinkle with remaining cheese.

4. Bake 13 to 15 minutes or until golden. Serve warm.

ঙ Deviled Eggs ৯

12 hard-cooked eggs

One 4.23-ounce can boneless skinned
    sardines

2 tablespoons finely minced green onions

½ teaspoon fresh savory

Salt

Juice of 1 lemon

½ teaspoon Worcestershire sauce

Mayonnaise, if necessary

Ripe olives and minced herbs, for garnish

1. Cool eggs quickly under cold running water. Shell and halve the long way. Remove
yolks carefully and mash.

2. Drain and mash sardines. Season sardines
with minced onion, savory, salt, lemon
juice, and Worcestershire sauce.

3. Beat mashed egg yolks into sardine mixture and taste for seasoning. If mixture
needs binding, blend in a little mayonnaise.

4. Using a spoon or knife, fill egg whites with
sardine mixture through a pastry tube using rosette attachment. Garnish each
stuffed egg with slices of ripe olives and
herbs. Makes 24 stuffed eggs.

ঙ Carol's Crab Ring ৯

1 teaspoon unflavored gelatin

¼ cup cold water

Two 8-ounce packages cream cheese, soft-
    ened

2 tablespoons cooking sherry

¾ teaspoon seasoned salt (optional)

One 2-ounce jar pimientos, sliced and
    drained

One 6-ounce package frozen king crabmeat,
    thawed, drained, and cut up

⅛ teaspoon freshly ground black pepper

¼ cup snipped fresh parsley

1. Sprinkle gelatin over water to soften. Stir
over hot water until smooth. Stir in next
six ingredients and 2 tablespoons of the
parsley. Pour into a 3-cup ring mold.

2. Refrigerate at least 4 hours or until set.
Serve out of mold or turn out onto a plate.
Garnish with remaining fresh parsley.
Serve with crackers. Makes 12 to 15 serv-
ings.

Identify hot dishes by marking them
with red carnations or whole red chili
peppers.

❧ Teresa's Savory Sausages ❧

Make plenty — these are popular!

1 pound little tiny sausage links (approximately 50 links) (or slice kielbasa)

½ cup currant jelly

1½ tablespoons fresh lemon juice

1½ teaspoons prepared mustard

½ cup chili sauce (or ¼ cup barbecue sauce)

1 teaspoon ground mustard

Dash cayenne pepper

One 20-ounce can cubed pineapple chunks with liquid

1. In a large saucepan, combine all ingredients. Simmer slowly until sauce thickens and becomes almost a glaze.

2. Reheat in a chafing dish and provide toothpicks to serve. Makes 12 servings.

❧ Dilled Olives ❧

1 clove garlic, crushed

½ teaspoon dill weed

One 9-ounce jar large pimiento-stuffed olives

Add garlic and dill weed to liquid in olives. Shake well. Store in refrigerator at least several days to season.

❧ Scott's Stuffed Clams ❧

1 medium onion, minced

1 clove garlic, pressed

1 teaspoon olive oil

1 cup minced clams with liquid

1 cup bread crumbs

1 teaspoon fresh lemon juice

2 tablespoons white wine

¼ cup grated Parmesan cheese

1 tablespoon minced fresh parsley

1 teaspoon dried oregano

Dash salt and freshly ground black pepper

Clam shells, brushed and cleaned

1. Preheat oven to 350°F.

2. Sauté onion and garlic in olive oil until golden brown. Add remaining ingredients, except shells, and mix well. Stuff into clam shells. Bake for 10 minutes and serve. Makes 18 small shells.

CHAPTER 14

Edible Flowers
for Fun and Flavor

*Lavender grey, lavender
    blue,
Perfume wrapt in the sky's
    own hue;
Lavender blue, lavender
    grey,
Love in memory lives always.*

*Lavender grey, lavender
    blue,
Sweet is remembrance if
    love be true;
Lavender blue, lavender
    grey,
Sweeter methinks, is the love
    of today.*

— Lady Lindsay

AFTER CENTURIES OF NEGLECT, edible flowers are finally taking the world by storm. This ancient medieval practice is the latest thing in cookery and now is featured in posh restaurants everywhere. You can use flowers as centerpieces, float them in drinking water, garnish plates and platters lavishly, and include them in the dish itself. Whether or not your guests are tempted to nibble on your flowers, use them anyway — with herbs, of course.

Select only unsprayed flowers, wash them well, cover them with plastic, and condition them by refrigerating (see pages 32–36). Supermarkets usually do not handle such perishables, and you must avoid florist flowers, as most have been sprayed.

Learn what's edible from your garden, then plan to use it at your bridal party. There is nothing lovelier than fresh purple lilacs tossed in a green salad or chicken salad served in bright pink tulip cups. Or, try red rose petal sandwiches on white bread, steam daylily buds as a special vegetable, or serve violet pinwheel sandwiches — always a hit.

The flowers and leaves of all culinary herbs are edible. Use them as seasonings or as garnishes liberally. Any of the following will dress your party: angelica, begonia, borage, burnet, calendula (pot marigold), camomile, capers, catnip, chives, clary sage, costmary, dill, fennel, hyssop, lavender, lemon balm, marjoram, mignonette, mints of all kinds, nasturtium, oregano, rosemary (especially the flowers, when available), saffron, sage, tansy, thyme, sweet woodruff, and violets.

SOME EDIBLE FLOWERS

Acacia flowers, golden yellow

Apple buds and blossoms, pretty pink

Banana blossoms, if you have any

Begonia, from the windowsill

Borage, bright blue stars, pieces of heaven

Broom and Scotch broom, in gold

Carnations and their cousins, the "pinks"

Chrysanthemums, spicy

Clovers, in assorted sizes and colors

Cornflowers or bachelor's-buttons

Cowslips, also known as primroses

Daisies, they won't tell

Dandelion, flowers, leaves, and roots

Daylilies, my favorite (including tiger lilies)

Elderflowers, for beauty

Hawthorne, blossoms or berries

Hollyhocks, to stuff

Honeysuckle, symbol of fraternal love

Jasmine, more fragrance

Johnny-jump-ups, Shakespeare's "heartsease"

Lemon, lime, or orange blossoms

Lilacs, in many colors

Lotus, exotic fare

Mallows, all the many mallows

Marigolds, especially lemon scented

Nasturtiums, in brilliant colors

Orchids, yes, orchids strewn lavishly on foods and in drinks

Pansies, "that's for thoughts"

Passion flowers, they last but a day

Peonies, petals or whole voluptuous blooms

Poppies, petals and seeds

Rose hips

Roses, the most lovesome flowers for weddings

Snapdragons, colorful little dragons

Squash blossoms, all varieties

Sunflowers, another daisy

Thistles, pretty, but handle carefully

Tulips, in delightful colors

Violets, candy them for Christmas

Yucca, pretty enough for a bride's bouquet and edible, too

❧ Candied Herbs and Flowers ❧

As garnishes, favors, or to decorate a pretty country-look cake with snowy white icing, these will be the hit of your party. Use mint leaves, fresh lavender flower spikes (see next recipe), violet flowers, rose petals, coriander seeds, or borage blossoms. Wash herbs of your choice, wrap in terry toweling, and then place in the refrigerator to crisp and dry.

1 egg white, beaten until frothy
Food coloring
1 cup granulated sugar

Dip your herb in beaten egg white (or colored egg white). Cover both sides carefully with sugar. Place on waxed paper-covered cookie sheets, as egg white will glue itself to anything else. (Don't even attempt to remove flower calyxes or you will have only petals.) Set aside to dry. This may take up to two weeks depending upon humidity. Makes 100 violets, 50 mint leaves, or 20 lavender spikes.

Candied borage flowers are a simple but lovely garnish.

❧ Lavender Sticks ❧

12 stalks fresh lavender flowers
1 egg white, beaten until frothy
½ cup granulated sugar

Dip lavender sprigs (flowers only) in egg white, then roll in or dust on sugar. Air-dry on waxed paper. Makes 1 dozen nibbles.

❧ Poppyseed Dressing ❧

⅓ cup fresh lemon juice
⅔ cup light corn syrup
¼ cup vegetable oil
1 tablespoon poppyseeds
⅛ teaspoon salt

Combine all ingredients, and shake vigorously to blend. Makes 1½ cups.

✑ Stuffed Nasturtiums ✎

1 cup cream cheese (8 ounces)

3 tablespoons mayonnaise

¼ cup chopped nuts

¼ cup grated carrots

1 tablespoon finely minced green bell pepper

2 teaspoons fresh basil, parsley, dill, or other herbs (or 2 tablespoons chives, cucumber, or green onion, minced)

1½ dozen brilliant nasturtium blossoms, washed

1. Soften cream cheese with mayonnaise. Add other ingredients, except blossoms.

2. Roll into balls, and fit into nasturtium flowers. Top with a bit of chives or any edible blossom.

3. Ring platter with round, bright green nasturtium leaves. Or, serve as individual salad garnishes, each on a leaf or two. Makes 18.

✑ Salad aux Fleurs ✎

2 heads assorted greens, red leaf lettuce, or endive

Edible flowers of your choice (see list on page 173 and illustration below)

Chopped fresh parsley, burnet, and chives for additional flavor

1. Wash and crisp lettuce by rolling it in clean dry toweling. Do the same with the flowers. (Use flowers from an unsprayed garden.)

2. Arrange the bed of greens on a large platter, then sprinkle with colorful flowers and the herbs.

3. Keep covered with plastic wrap, and refrigerate until ready to serve. Serve with *Poppyseed Dressing.* Makes 10 to 12 servings.

Some edible flowers: (clockwise from top left) nasturtiums, daylily, johnny-jump-ups, chives, begonia, violets, calendula.

❧ *Violet Jelly* ❧

Collect small, pretty glasses or baby food jars to make this for a decorative favor. Brandy snifters are attractive. For a rich violet color, pick lots of violets in season. The more flowers you steep, the richer the purple color. This jelly makes a jewel-like garnish for any party plate.

1 quart violet blossoms
Boiling water
Juice of 1 lemon
1 box of fruit pectin
4 cups granulated sugar

♥

Blue Violets symbolize Faithfulness.
Dame Violets for Watchfulness.
Sweet Violets are for Modesty.
Yellow Violets stand for Rural
Happiness.

1. Fill a quart jar with violet blossoms, and cover with boiling water. Steep for 24 hours. Strain.

2. To 2 cups of this liquid, add juice of 1 lemon and 1 box of fruit pectin. Bring to a boil and add 4 cups sugar. Bring again to a boil, and boil hard for 1 minute.

3. Ladle into sterilized glass jars and seal with paraffin. Or, freeze in rigid plastic containers with lids. Makes 5 cups.

❧ *Violet Pinwheels* ❧

Be sure to serve these pretty-as-a-picture sandwiches whenever violets are in bloom. It is truly a showpiece. It also makes a delicious tea party dish. (Color photo, page 94.)

1. Use softened cream cheese, mixed with minced fresh chives, thyme, parsley, lemon balm, and/or tarragon. Spread on thin-sliced white bread. Cover with violets, and roll up. Refrigerate each roll, wrapped in a paper towel, in a covered dish.

2. To serve, cut each roll into 5 pinwheels with scissors, and place on a silver tray with lace paper doilies. Top each little pinwheel with a fresh violet blossom, and serve immediately. Ten slices of bread make 50 pinwheels.

Rose-Petal Sandwiches

8 slices white bread

One 3-ounce package cream cheese, softened

1 tablespoon rose water

4 drops red food coloring (optional)

4 full-blown red roses, washed with petals separated

1. Remove crusts from bread. Cream cheese with rose water, and tint it light pink, if desired. Spread one side of each slice of bread with cheese mixture. Cover four of the slices with separated rose petals. Be sure each petal touches cream cheese, so that sandwiches adhere. Wrap tightly in plastic wrap, and refrigerate.

2. Before serving, cut each whole sandwich in half. Cut each half into four or five pieces. Arrange pieces around edge of a pretty plate, cut side up to show the ribbon of red roses. Center with several matching roses, leaves, and buds. Makes 32 to 40 dainty tea sandwiches. (Color photo, page 94.)

For a most romantic touch, spike the white wine punch with delicate violet blossoms. Floating in the punch bowl or waiting in empty glasses, these signs of spring will make your heart sing.

Postlude

If all this seems like much ado about "I do," bear in mind the awesome significance of a wedding — it's fully a lifetime commitment. Such a quantum leap forward pours excess adrenaline into the body, all of it demanding to be put to good use. The many extra little herbal projects in *Herbs for Weddings and Other Celebrations* will satisfy your need to be busy and creative. Given plenty of time, you can express yourself by personally designing your wedding with careful attention to all details.

As the date approaches and excitement mounts, the pace quickens. There's much to be said for making bows, stuffing baskets with herb arrangements, gluing pressed herbs on place cards, folding fancy flared napkins, freezing pretty ice rings of herbs for the parties, all touched by love.

Each and every idea scratched off endless lists well in advance means precious last-minute time to enjoy your party and play along with your guests. Pamper yourself! Then don your wedding gown, and join your families and friends in all the justified and carefree festivities.

A word of caution: Although you can do it all by yourself if you want to, I would advise against such folly. There are enough ideas in *Herbs for Weddings and Other Celebrations* to keep a dozen brides and their families and friends busy planning their weddings and peripheral parties. And, don't forget the anniversaries to come, when *Herbs for Weddings and Other Celebrations* will prove indispensable.

Be selective. Don't hesitate to parcel out projects to talented friends or professionals. Smart planning and detailed lists, teamwork, and cooperation assure you a picture-perfect day to remember.

When you are at last altar bound to the jubilant strains of Wagner or other fanfare, radiantly beautiful, carrying a bouquet redolent of fragrant herbs, think of their ancient symbolism. Herbs don't shout, they whisper — a romantic sonnet that will sustain you for a lifetime of wedded bliss.

A herbal wedding will do just that. The secret lies in good planning along with a little effort and simple ingenuity using herbs. Herbs make all the difference in the world.

Love suffereth long, and is kind ; Love envieth not ; Love vaunteth not itself, is not puffed-up, doth not behave itself unseemly, seeketh not her own, is not easily provoked, thinketh no evil ; Rejoiceth not in iniquity, but rejoiceth in the truth ; Beareth all things, believeth all things, hopeth all things, endureth all things.
Love never faileth.
And now abideth faith, hope, love, these three ;
But the greatest of these is love.

1 Corinthians 13th chapter

Mail-Order Sources

Many of the supplies needed for projects in this book are available at local craft stores, herb shops, grocery stores, or florists. If you can't find materials locally, call or write to these mail-order suppliers.

Fresh-Cut Herbs and Edible Flowers

Write first for current information.

Bay Laurel Farm
Glory H. Condon
West Garzas Road
Carmel Valley, CA 93924
408-659-2913

Price list, $2

Florida Edible Flowers
Michael and Mary Shallies
6005 Tenth Avenue, NW
Naples, FL 33999
813-598-4552

Fox Hill Farm
Marilyn Hampstead
444 W. Michigan Avenue, Box 9
Parma, MI 49269
517-531-3179

Free list

Herb Gathering, Inc.
Paula A. Winchester
5742 Kenwood Avenue
Kansas City, MO 64110
816-523-2653

Quail Mountain Herbs
P.O. Box 1049
Watsonville, CA 95077
408-722-8456

Taylor's Herb Garden
Jean Langley
P.O. Box 362
Congress, AZ 85332
602-427-3201
Wholesale only

Valihai Herbs
Mark Dayley
214 East 34th Street
Boise, ID 83714
208-376-HERB

Other Accessories

Arts and Flowers of Cider Hill Farm
Sarah and Gary Milek
R.R. 1, Box 1066
Windsor, VT 05089
802-674-5293

To order a symbolic wedding herb print to frame or to use as very handy notepapers.

Dorothy Biddle Service
HC01 Box 900
Greeley, PA 18425-9799
717-226-3239

For floral foam products and flower arranging supplies; free catalog.

Maid of Scandinavia
3244 Raleigh Avenue
Minneapolis, MN 55416
1-800-328-6722

For heart-shaped doilies, tier cake pans, wedding bells galore, strings of pearls, and a bride's "lucky sixpence" for her shoe.

Pine Creek Herbs
Kathleen M. Gips
152 South Main Street
Chagrin Falls, OH 44022
216-247-5014

For "The Language of Flowers" (a dictionary of floral lore) and a catalog listing sentimental accessories.

The Rosemary House, Inc.
120 S. Market Street
Mechanicsburg, PA 17055
717-697-5111

For mint molds, extracts, wedding rice, and other helpful herbal items, such as wreath or herbal craft books and supplies, 'Fairy' roses, Flower-Dri, "Rosemary for Remembrance" sampler to embroider, "Wreaths...of all sorts" booklet, etc. Catalog $2.00.

Further Reading

Bernath, Stefen. *Herbs Coloring Book*. Mineola, NY: Dover Publications, 1977 (up to four herbs may be used free for each project).

Duff, Gail. *Natural Fragrances*. Pownal, VT: Garden Way Publishing, 1989.

Genders, Roy. *Flowers and Herbs of Love*. England: Darton, Longman and Todd, 1978.

Gips, Kathleen M. *The Language of Flowers*. Chagrin Falls, OH: 1990 (complete dictionary of Victorian floral sentiments).

Jacobs, Betty E. M. *Flowers that Last Forever*. Pownal, VT: Garden Way Publishing, 1988.

Jacobs, Betty E. M. *Growing and Using Herbs Successfully*. Pownal, VT: Garden Way Publishing, 1981.

Marcin, Marietta Marshall. *The Herbal Tea Garden*. Pownal, VT: Garden Way Publishing, 1993.

Newman, John G. *The Ladies' Flora*. London: L.L. Boardman & Co., 1854.

Picksten, Margaret. *The Language of Flowers*. London: Waterlows, 1968 (copy of 1913 handwritten book).

Language of Flowers, illustrated by Kate Greenaway. New York: Merrimack Publishing Corp., originally published in 1884.

The Language of Flowers, with illustrations by Redoute. Philadelphia: Running Press, 1991 (a miniature edition).

Selam. *Oriental Language of Flowers*.

Shaudys, Phyllis, V. *Herbal Treasures*. Pownal, VT: Garden Way Publishing, 1990.

Shaudys, Phyllis, V. *The Pleasure of Herbs*. Pownal, VT: Garden Way Publishing, 1986.

Recipe Index

Page numbers in italics indicate illustrations.

General Index

Page numbers in italics indicate illustrations.

H

Hair combs, 52, *97*
Hair ornaments, 49-50, *50*
Hardening herbs, 32-36
Hats, trimming straw, 87, *87*
Hawthorne, 173
    meaning of, 105
Heart bouquets, 48-49, *48*
Heart cakes, 133, *133*
Heart sachets, 83-84, *83*
Heather, meaning of, 102
Heliotrope, meaning of, 105
Herbal halos, 50, *50*, 97
Herbs
    conditioning/hardening,
      32-36
    labeling, 14
    where to obtain, 3-4,
      181-82
Hibiscus tea, 157
Holly, meaning of, 105
Hollyhocks, 173
Honesty, meaning of, 105
Honeysuckle, 173
    meaning of, 105
Hoop bouquets, 36, *37*
House, how to make a
    miniature, 13-14, *13*
Hyacinth, meaning of, 105
Hyssop, meaning of, 105

I

Ice-cream cone sachets, 81,
    81
Ice ring, 159
Invitations
    framed wedding, 77-78, 93
    how to make, 73-74, *73,*
      74

ideas for, 15, 23-24
Iris, meaning of, 105
Ivy, meaning of, 105
Ivy wreath, meaning of, 102

J

Jasmine, 173
    meaning of, 102, 105
Jasminum sabue. See Jasmine
Johnny-jump-ups, *143*, 173,
    175
    meaning of, 105
Juniper, meaning of, 105

K

Kneeling bench, 17

L

Lace
    how to use, 6-9
    making nosegays from,
      7-8, *8*
Lad's-love, meaning of, 105
Lamb's-ears, *103*
    meaning of, 103
Larkspur, meaning of, 102
Lavender, *81*
    favor, *94,* 107
    how to use, 81
    meaning of, 102, 103, 105
    recipes using, 174
Lemon
    meaning of, 105
    recipes using, 121, 136,
      141-42, 148, 151, 154,
      161
Lemon balm, *11*
    how to use, 10-11

meaning of, 105, 106
Lemon verbena, *147*
    meaning of, 105
Lighting, use of, 113
Lilacs, 173
    meaning of, 104, 105
Lily-of-the-Valley, meaning
    of, 102, 105
Linden blossoms, meaning of,
    103, 105
Lollipop, 81, *81*
Lotus, 173
Lovage, *160*
Lover's knot, 100
Lunaria, meaning of, 105,
    106

M

Mail-order sources, 181-82
Mallows, 173
Marigolds, 173
Marjoram, meaning of, 102,
    105
Meadowsweet, meaning of,
    105
Melissa officinalis. See Lemon
    balm
Menu planning, 26
Mignonette, meaning of, 105
Milek, Gary, 102, 104
Milk-glass containers, white,
    62
Mint, 17, *29, 145*
    meaning of, 105
    recipes using, 121, 135,
      145, 148, 150, 157
Mirrors, use of, 113
Moneyplant, 106
Mugwort, meaning of, 105

Mullein, meaning of, 103
Mushroom baskets, 61
Mustard seed, meaning of, 105
Myrtle, *32*
   how to use, 21
   meaning of, 31-32, 101, 105
Myrtus communis. See Myrtle

N

Napkins, how to fold, 115-117, *115, 117*
Nasturtiums, 173, *175*
   meaning of, 105
   recipe using, 175
Nigella, meaning of, 102
Nosegays
   herbs for, 37, 41
   how to make, 38-41, *38, 41*
   from lace, 7-8, *8*
   sachet, 81

O

Olive, meaning of, 105
Orange blossom, *32*
   how to use, 31
   meaning of, 32, 100, 105
Orchids, 173
Oregano, meaning of, 105
Oriental Language of Flowers (Selam), 104
Orrisroot, 78

P

Pansies, 173
   meaning of, 104, 105
Parkinson, John, 101

Parsley, *29*
   how to use, 5
   meaning of, 103, 105
   recipe using, 167
Passion flowers, 173
Pearly everlasting, meaning of, 103
Peonies, 173
Peppermint, *153*
   meaning of, 105
   tea, 157
Pew bows, 55-56, *55*
Photographs, herbal vignettes, 16
Picnics, 22-24
Picture frames, 15
Pikake, meaning of, 102
Pinks, meaning of, 105
Place cards, 73-74, *73, 74*
Ponderosa lemon tree, 32
Poppies, 173
Poppyseeds, recipes using, 137-38, 168, 174
Posies
   pocket, 54
   spice, 24-25, *24*
Potpourri, 77-78
   parasols, 82-83, *82*
   recipes for, 79
Prayer book, herbs on, 43, *43*
Pressed flowers, 77
Primroses, 173
Progressive dinner party, 23
Punch bowls, wreaths around, 59

Q

Queen-Anne's-lace
   how to use, 8-9

meaning of, 105

R

Receptions, 59-64
Ribbon roses, 67, *67*
Rice, custom of throwing, 88-89
Rice roses, 89-90, *90*
Ring bearer's pillow, 16, 85-86, *86*
Rings, symbolism of, 12-13
Romanwood plant, meaning of, 103, 106
Rose-filled ice ring, how to make, 159
Rose hips, *123*, 173
   recipes using, 123, 157
Rosemary, *5*
   on announcements, 20-21
   how to use, 5-6, 31
   meaning of, 5-6, 32, 101, 102, 103, 105
   topiaries, 15
Rose petals, 16-17
   basket of, *97*
   recipes using, *94*, 177
Roses, 173
   meaning of, 102, 103, 105
Rue, *103*
   meaning of, 103, 105

S

Sachet(s)
   bride's heels, 84-85, *84*
   centerpieces, 80-81
   favors, 80
   ice-cream cone, 81, *81*
   keepsake, 80
   lollipop, 81, *81*